FEARLESS FIRSTS

ATHLETES
WHO CHANGED THE
GAME

WRITTEN BY
JAMES BUCKLEY JR. & ELLEN LABRECQUE

PICTURES BY
STEFFI WALTHALL

sourcebooks
eXplore

Table of Contents

Introduction

Sports are all about finishing first. But what if you're not even allowed to get in the game? For many decades, lots of people were prevented from taking part because of their skin color, their gender, their abilities, their sexuality, and more. Things have changed, and today's sports world is—with a few exceptions—diverse, inclusive, and accepting. It's not perfect, but it has come a long way. In this book, we'll celebrate the people who helped create that change, the athletes who broke barriers, took risks, and pushed back against injustice. They had to put up with abuse and ignorance. They were forced to fight for what they deserved. And they used courage to stand up and create pathways to the future.

The great Jackie Robinson, who in 1947 became the first Black player in Major League Baseball in the twentieth century, was the inspiration for this book. His story is here, on page 78. But as we looked at what Jackie did, we saw that he was far from alone. Some of the people who followed him are nearly as well-known as he was: Roberto Clemente, Serena Williams, and Simone Biles. A few athletes who broke barriers *before* Jackie are well-known too: Major Taylor, Jim Thorpe, and Babe Didrikson Zaharias. You'll find lots of books and videos about those courageous superstars.

But the world of sports is huge and packed with stories from every field, arena, gym, pool, track, and stadium. That's what this book is about—finding room for lots more firsts from the world of sports. Who was the first female drag-racing champion? Who was the first Olympic gymnast who won a gold medal with only one leg? Who was the first Hispanic female pro golfer? What was the first Indigenous team welcomed to international sports? Jackie Robinson was, famously, the first Black professional baseball player. But what about the first Black players in pro baseball, football, and hockey? Find out how a racer with bipolar disorder succeeds. Watch how a Mexican American golfer can break par *and* barriers. See how women are blazing trails in the sports business. Learn about groundbreaking LGBTQIA+ athletes.

The world of sports, more than ever before, has room in the lineup for everyone! There is still lots of work to be done, but we hope the examples from this book inspire athletes today...and in the future...to keep working hard to knock down any barriers that stand in their way.

A Century (Plus!) of Firsts

Most of the people you'll meet in this book accomplished their barrier-breaking feats in the twentieth century. Those one hundred years (plus a few on either side of the century) saw sports grow from a few local contests into international spectacles. New sports were invented, new leagues started, and new global contests created. Without all these famous firsts, our Fearless Firsters would not have had anywhere to play!

1875
First Kentucky Derby race

1891
Dr. James Naismith invented basketball

1896
First Summer Olympics

1897
First Boston Marathon race

1902
First Rose Bowl game

1903
First World Series
First Tour de France bicycle race

1911
First Indy 500 race

1917
First National Hockey League (NHL) game

1920
First National Football League (NFL) game

The league was first called the American Professional Football Association from 1920 to 1921.

1924
First Winter Olympics

1930
First World Cup of soccer

1946
First Basketball Association of America game

The BAA merged with the National Basketball League to form today's National Basketball Association (NBA) in 1950.

1950
First Ladies Professional Golf Association (LPGA) tournament, the Tampa Women's Open

1959
First Daytona 500 race

1960
First Paralympic Games

1967
First Super Bowl game

1968
First Special Olympics Summer Games

1978
First Ironman Race

1991
First Women's World Cup of soccer

1995
First X Games

1996
First Major League Soccer (MLS) game

1997
First Women's National Basketball Association (WNBA) game
First Winter X Games

2013
First National Women's Soccer League (NWSL) game

JIM ABBOTT

First MLB Pitcher born with One Hand

———

BORN 1967

Baseball coaches tell young players from the first day of practice: "Use two hands to catch the ball!" But what if you don't have two hands? That was the problem Jim Abbott faced—and overcame.

Jim was born in Michigan in 1967 without a right hand. Even though his parents suggested soccer, where missing a hand is not a big deal, Jim was determined to play baseball like his friends. He soon became one of the top pitchers in his youth leagues. But how?

Working with his dad, Jim learned a super quick way to throw and catch with the same hand. He rested his fielding glove on the stump of his right arm. As soon as he released the ball with his left hand, he switched the glove onto it. If the ball came zinging back toward him, he caught it, flipped it in the air, dropped the glove, grabbed the ball, and threw it. He could do all that in less than one second!

In high school, Jim was a quarterback and punter for the football team. He pitched in baseball, but he also hit—one-handed, batting .427 with seven homers one season. His talent earned him a spot at the University of Michigan, where he kept pitching and winning. The Wolverines won the Big Ten title twice.

In 1987, after receiving the Golden Spikes Award as the top college baseball player, Jim was the first baseball player ever to be given the Sullivan Award as the country's top amateur athlete. He then skipped minor-league baseball and joined the California Angels in 1989, the first one-handed pitcher in modern major-league history. (History fans: Pete Gray was not a pitcher, but he played one season of Major League Baseball in the 1940s with just one arm. Look him up!)

With the Angels, Jim became a national sensation. Fans flocked to watch him. Fellow players were impressed with his skill and courage. People with similar disabilities were inspired while watching him pitch. And he was pretty good. The best of his ten major-league seasons came in 1991, when he was 18–11 and finished third in voting for the Cy Young Award.

The highlight of Jim's career came on September 4, 1993, when he pitched a no-hitter while winning a game for the New York Yankees. But Jim's bigger highlight has been encouraging young fans to dream big too.

TINA AMENT

First Blind Ironman Finisher

——

BORN 1962

When Tina Ament was born, she had a genetic eye condition that made her blind. Her sister was born with the same condition. Unlike the culture around her, Tina's parents did not think their daughters' situations were something to feel sorry about.

"My parents would not put up with that," Tina said.

Throughout her childhood, Tina swam, rode horseback, and skied in the mountains. Then she began rowing and even rowed in college. Through rowing, she met endurance athletes and discovered that was what she wanted to do. She finished her first marathon in 2006 and her first triathlon in 2010.

A few years later, Tina competed in the 2014 Ironman world championship in Hawaii. This race is one of the most grueling in the world. It begins with a 2.4-mile swim, which is followed by a 112-mile bike ride, and concludes with a 26.2-mile run. Whenever she races, Tina rides tandem with a sighted guide on a bike and then is tethered to her partner by a rope for swimming and running. In Hawaii, they battled choppy waves during the swim and faced strong winds on the bike and run.

"We got to someplace around Mile 17 of the run, and I was like, 'Oh no, we still have nine miles to go,'" Tina said. "There were some moments of panic there."

But Tina just kept running. She crossed the finish line in 16 hours, 18 minutes, and 5 seconds. She became the first blind woman ever to complete this race, and she is now an eight-time Ironman finisher.

Then in the summer of 2018, Tina was part of the first team with limited vision that competed in Race Across America. Her team, Sea to See, biked 3,100 miles from Oceanside, California, to Annapolis, Maryland, over the course of one week.

But the team wasn't just riding for fun. They were raising awareness for businesses to hire more blind employees. More than 70 percent of people with vision loss in the United States are jobless. Since Tina works as a lawyer in Washington, DC, this issue is very important to her.

"As a blind person, we are constantly figuring out how to do something, not thinking about why we can't," Tina said. "We want everybody to think about blind people in that same way too. We can do anything we set our minds to—we just need to be given a chance."

RACHEL BALKOVEC

First Woman to Manage a Pro Baseball Team

———

BORN 1987

When Rachel Balkovec walked onto the field with the lineup card for the Tampa Tarpons on April 8, 2022, she made history. She was officially the first woman to manage a minor-league baseball team.

Rachel had grown up in Nebraska loving softball...and watching baseball. She played softball in high school and college, and she had male friends on college baseball teams who she watched advance to life in the pros. Rachel wanted to follow her pro sports dream too, but pro softball was not big enough for her to make a living, and women were almost never part of baseball's coaching ranks.

But that didn't stop Rachel.

Her first move was to become a strength coach—helping athletes get stronger in the weight room. In 2014, she became baseball's first minor-league female strength and conditioning coach with the St. Louis Cardinals. After also working with the Houston Astros, Rachel had bigger plans: she aimed to become a hitting coach. After Rachel spent years practicing and studying, including months in the Netherlands learning about biomechanics, the New York Yankees hired her in 2019.

Rachel became the first female hitting coach in the minor leagues.

In 2020, minor-league baseball was canceled due to COVID-19, so Rachel flew to Australia to help coach in a pro league there. Before the 2022 season, the Yankees saw how far she'd come and named her the manager of their Class A minor-league Tarpons.

The news got national attention from inside and outside the world of baseball. Fans piled onto Rachel's Instagram to say congratulations. Articles about her barrier-breaking new job appeared all over. Once the dust settled, Rachel got to work. In her first game, the Tarpons won 9–6, although you could say that the game of baseball was the real winner in this contest.

Rachel is the most famous of a growing number of women working in pro baseball. Alyssa Nakken filled in as the first female on-field coach in the major leagues in a 2022 game for the San Francisco Giants. And Kim Ng (page 64) became the first female MLB general manager in 2021. Who knows? The next big move might be a woman *playing* in the pros!

SIMONE BILES

First Female Gymnast to Win Four Olympic Golds

———

BORN 1997

Simone Biles has established herself as the most dynamic gymnast in the history of her sport. She won three world all-around titles in a row from 2013 to 2015. Then at the 2016 Olympics in Rio de Janeiro, when she was just nineteen years old, she became the first American female gymnast to win four gold medals in a single Olympics. Simone also led the Americans to the team gold. On the vault and floor exercise, the explosive four-foot-eight-inch gymnast flew higher through the air and performed more difficult feats than fans had ever thought possible.

Simone returned to lead her team at the 2020 Olympics in Tokyo. But to everyone's surprise, she withdrew from the team's final events. Simone revealed that she was dealing with the "twisties"—a condition that prevents gymnasts from knowing where they are in the air. If a gymnast competes with the twisties, they could end up seriously injuring themselves.

She decided to put her mental health ahead of her desire to compete. After withdrawing, Simone spoke out about the pressures that elite athletes face and the toll this can take on their mental health. She wanted to help others by being honest about her own condition.

"We have to protect our mind and our body, rather than just go out there and do what the world wants us to do," Simone said. "I do hope that people can relate and understand it's OK to not be OK—and it's OK to talk about it," she said.

At the Tokyo games, Simone returned for the final event, the balance beam, where she won the bronze medal. This was her seventh Olympic medal, tying her for the most won by any American gymnast ever.

In July 2022, Simone was awarded the Presidential Medal of Freedom by the White House. This is the highest honor a civilian can receive. Simone was honored for her gymnastics achievements but also for her work for mental health and safety. Simone, who was twenty-five at the time, was the youngest person ever to receive the award.

Simone helped others by sharing her fears and speaking out about the importance of mental health. Over a year later, in August 2023, Simone won a record eighth U.S. Championship title—the most of any gymnast ever. She was given a standing ovation at the competition, not just because of her performance on the mat, but because she helped others by sharing her fears and speaking out about the importance of mental health. This makes her the GOAT (greatest of all time) in more ways than one.

ROBERTO CLEMENTE

First Latin American Baseball Superstar

1934–1972

Although baseball has been popular in the Spanish-speaking countries of Central and South America and in the Caribbean since the 1800s, players from these regions did not get a chance to play in the major leagues in the United States for decades. A few Spanish speakers had reached the majors, but they were all light-skinned. Sadly, dark-skinned Hispanic men were kept out of baseball because of their skin color and the language they spoke. The ban against Black players ended in 1947, thanks to Jackie Robinson (page 78), and in 1949, Orestes "Minnie" Miñoso from Cuba became the first Afro-Latino ballplayer in the majors.

But while Miñoso opened the door slightly, Puerto Rico's Roberto Clemente would kick it wide open. Blessed with speed, a rocket right arm, and outstanding batting skills, Roberto was discovered in 1954 at a tryout for players on his home island. The Brooklyn Dodgers then signed him for a minor-league team.

While playing in the minors, Roberto had to learn English and battle racism. When his team competed in the South, he was excluded from some restaurants and hotels. He faced the same problem in Florida, playing for the Pittsburgh Pirates. The media didn't make Spanish-speaking players feel welcome either. The newspapers would quote Roberto saying "beeg leegs" for big leagues or "heet" for hit. They even called him Bobby, not Roberto!

But Roberto kept plugging away, improving his game and his English.

Soon, Roberto became one of the top players in the league and helped the Pirates win the 1960 World Series. For the next decade, he piled up award after award, including the 1966 National League Most Valuable Player (MVP) and four batting titles. In 1971, he was the World Series MVP when the Pirates secured another championship.

Through it all, Roberto inspired a generation of players from Spanish-speaking countries who also helped change baseball. In recent seasons, more than 30 percent of MLB players have been from these regions.

Roberto's story began and ended with courage. He used his well-earned fame to help people back in Puerto Rico speak out for civil rights. In 1972, he was tragically killed in a plane crash while helping deliver supplies to Nicaragua after an earthquake. Today, MLB gives an award named for Roberto Clemente to the player who best combines skills and community service.

JASON COLLINS

First Openly Gay Male Athlete in a Major American Sport

———

BORN 1979

When men began playing team sports in the United States professionally, the idea of a gay man being part of the team was never talked about. Any players who were gay never said so, in part because coming out of the closet was very difficult in most places. In other places, it was against the law.

As the antigay biases and laws began to change, a few players revealed *after* their playing careers that they were, in fact, gay. But it was not until 2013 that an *active* American major-sport athlete came out. In April 2013, Jason Collins wrote in *Sports Illustrated*, "I'm a 34-year-old NBA center. I'm black. And I'm gay." The announcement sent shock waves through the NBA and sports. The reaction was mostly positive. President Barack Obama praised Jason, while NBA legend Magic Johnson and superstar Kobe Bryant also sent their support. Some players and media were against Jason, citing their religious beliefs. But as Jason knew, it was time.

Jason grew up in Los Angeles, where he was a high school star on the court and in the classroom. At Stanford University, he had been an All-American player and teammate of his (almost) equally tall twin brother, Jarron, who had his own successful NBA career. In 2013, Jason was near the end of what would become an eleven-season NBA career with six teams, including eight years with the New Jersey (now Brooklyn) Nets. Jason had known for a long time he was gay, but while he didn't feel comfortable saying so in public yet, he used other ways to show support for his community. For example, he wore the number 98 to remember Matthew Shepard, a young gay man killed in 1998. After Jason's announcement in 2014, his No. 98 was one of the biggest-selling souvenir jerseys in the NBA.

Though Jason retired after playing one more season with the Brooklyn Nets, he became a popular speaker about LGBTQIA+ issues. He still works for the NBA in community relations.

In 2021, Carl Nassib of the Las Vegas Raiders became the first openly gay player in the NFL. Luke Prokop, drafted by the NHL's Nashville Predators in 2020, also came out in 2021. No other NBA players have publicly come out as of yet.

14

ERNIE DAVIS

First Black Heisman Trophy Winner

———

1939–1963

The first Heisman Trophy, given each season to the best college football player, was awarded in 1935. Although Black players were part of some college teams—though none in the South—it would be twenty-six years before a Black player held up the Heisman in triumph.

That player was Ernie Davis. Ernie grew up in Elmira, New York, and was an outstanding athlete in several sports, including football. Several big colleges wanted him to play for them, but he chose Syracuse University, not far from his hometown.

One big reason Ernie went to Syracuse was another pioneering Black player, Jim Brown. Jim had starred with the Orangemen from 1954 to 1956 before moving to the NFL's Cleveland Browns. He saw Ernie's potential and told him what he would experience as a rare Black player at a mostly white school and on a mostly white team. It would not be easy, Jim said, but he thought Ernie had the inner strength to make it work.

In 1959, his first season playing, Ernie led Syracuse to a 10–0 record. The team earned a spot in the Cotton Bowl in Dallas, where they took on the University of Texas. Sadly, Syracuse's Black players reported that the Texas players spit on them and called them racist names. But Ernie persevered. He caught an 87-yard touchdown pass, ran four yards for another score, and even made a key interception while playing defense! The win helped Syracuse stay undefeated, and earn the school's first and only national championship in football.

In 1961, Ernie ran for 15 touchdowns and 823 rushing yards, and on December 6, he was announced as the winner of the Heisman Trophy. While he was in New York City for the award ceremony, Ernie met with President John F. Kennedy, and it was President Kennedy who had asked for the meeting, not Ernie. In three seasons at Syracuse, Ernie broke Jim Brown's school records for rushing yards and touchdowns, and impressed everyone with his maturity and positive attitude.

It looked like Ernie would follow Jim to the NFL and pro football success. In the 1962 NFL draft, he became the first Black player chosen first overall. Sadly, in May 1962, Ernie was diagnosed with leukemia. He never got to play in the NFL and died a year later when he was only twenty-three. Ernie's short life had a big impact, however, and he is remembered for his skill on the field and his courage off it.

MO'NE DAVIS

First Black Female Player in the Little League World Series

BORN 2001

The phrase "You throw like a girl" used to be thought of as an insult. It really meant "You can't throw a ball fast or well." But that has changed—especially since the world met Mo'ne Davis.

Mo'ne Davis was thirteen years old in the summer of 2014. She was the only girl on her team, which made it all the way to the Little League World Series. Only sixteen teams—eight from the United States and eight from countries around the world—make it to the series.

Her male teammates accepted "Mo" as one of their own. She was one of the team's star pitchers. Mo's fastball was clocked at over 70 miles per hour, and she also had a wicked curveball. It fooled batters and made them look like they were swinging with their eyes closed.

Soon after Mo'ne became the first Black girl to play in the Little League World Series, she became the first girl in series history to pitch her team to victory, shutting out Nashville 4–0. Mo'ne struck out eight batters in six innings in that game.

Mo'ne became an instant sensation—not just for her mad skills but for her cool and calm demeanor in the spotlight. "I always wanted to be a role model, but being a *baseball* role model is really cool," she said.

Professional athletes tweeted praise about Mo'ne. She was even invited to the White House to meet President Barack Obama and First Lady Michelle Obama. The First Couple told Mo'ne, "You changed the sports world. Keep going. Don't let anybody stop you."

Mo'ne took those words to heart. In the summer of 2015, she and her baseball teammates took a bus tour around the southern United States. The team played exhibition games, but more importantly, they toured historical sites where Black people had marched, protested, and lost their lives in the struggle for civil rights. The trip left Mo'ne saddened by the country's history of racial injustice but also "thankful for all the people who fought for the freedom we now have," she said.

Mo'ne chose to attend Hampton University, a historically Black college in Virgina, where she played second base for the softball team.

Mo'ne also earned a full scholarship to attend graduate school at Columbia University, where she studies sports management.

"I always believed that nobody can tell you you can't do something," Mo'ne said. "This world is huge, and there is so much space for everyone to do something great."

GABBY DOUGLAS

First Black Olympic All-Around Champion

———

BORN 1995

Gabby Douglas was born to be a gymnast. After all, she was doing one-handed cartwheels when she was a toddler. She was a Virginia state champion by age eight. When she was fourteen, Gabby moved from Virginia to Iowa to train full-time.

Just two years after moving, Gabby made Olympic history. At the 2012 Games in London, England, she became the first woman of color of any country and the first African American gymnast to become the individual all-around champion. She also became the first American gymnast to win gold in both the individual all-around and team competitions at the same games.

Gabby was known for her positive attitude. Her former coach Kittia Carpenter said, "That's her—always bubbly and energetic. That's part of what separates her from everyone else."

Gabby was also nicknamed the "Flying Squirrel" because she flew so high off the uneven bars for her dismount. This nickname was a compliment, but the other names people called Gabby were not. She dealt with racist bullies saying terrible things about her online and behind her back. People made fun of her hair and even the way she smiled or didn't smile.

"I was getting racist jokes," Gabby said. "I would come home at night and just cry my eyes out."

Gabby wanted to quit at times, but she knew that she could not let this type of behavior derail her dreams. She continued to compete and held her head high. At the 2016 Olympics, Gabby again helped her team win gold. But soon after the games, Gabby retired. She then decided to tell her story and help other kids who might have also been bullied along the way.

"I was tired of talking about the harassment, tired of crying," Gabby said. "I decided I was done feeling sorry for myself. Instead, I actually wanted to do something about it."

That is exactly what Gabby did. She became a national spokesperson to stop bullying—especially on the internet. She visits high schools and colleges around the country in hopes of helping other victims of bullying.

"I'm so glad that I'm talking about it now," Gabby said. "It makes me feel a whole lot better. You have to talk it out. I want to show people that no matter how bad it gets, you can do something about it."

VICKI MANALO DRAVES AND SAMMY LEE

First Asian American Olympic Gold Medalists

VICTORIA: 1924–2010; SAMMY: 1920–2016

Victoria "Vicki" Manalo Draves and Sammy Lee made history together and would also become lifelong friends. During the 1948 Olympics in London, England, these two divers became the first Asian Americans to win Olympic gold medals. Vicki won gold in the ten-meter platform and the three-meter springboard. Sammy won gold in the platform event and bronze on the springboard.

Vicki grew up in San Francisco, California. Her father was Filipino, and her mother was English. Sammy grew up in Los Angeles, California. His mother and father were of Korean descent. Although they didn't know each other, Vicki and Sammy both faced racism as kids because of their Asian backgrounds. Sammy was only allowed to swim at his public pool on "colored days," and for Vicki, the discrimination was just as bad.

"She would actually go to a pool and compete, and after she got done with the meet, they would empty the water out of the pool," Vicki's son, David Draves, said later about his mom's experience. "This really hurt my mom." At one point, Vicki was told to use her mother's maiden name, Taylor, instead of her own last name, Manalo, to hide the fact that she was Asian.

Vicki and Sammy met at the 1944 Amateur Athletic Union championships and immediately became pals. Sammy introduced Vicki to a new coach, Lyle Draves, who later became her husband. Sammy was the best man at their wedding.

After their history-making 1948 Olympic performances, Vicki traveled around the country and put on diving shows with other performers. Sammy continued to compete and won another gold medal on the 10-meter platform at the 1952 Games in Helsinki, Finland.

Both divers were inducted into the International Swimming Hall of Fame in the late 1960s. And although they remained very proud of their gold medals, it was not just because they were the first Asian Americans to win them.

"It was for yourself, but it was for your country, your family, as well," Sammy said about winning gold. "The Olympic Games are something different, because it's you and our system against the world."

Eventually, the two Olympians settled near each other in Southern California. Sammy became an Olympic diving coach and medical doctor. And Vicki and her husband opened a swimming and diving program where competitors of all races were always welcome.

An Important Law: TITLE IX

In 1972, a new law was passed in the United States. Called the Education Amendments Act, it was aimed at making education in the United States more equal between men and women. At the time, for example, only 8 percent of American women had college degrees. You read that right: 8 percent. But that was the tip of the iceberg of a century-plus of discrimination. More than a million more men than women went to college in 1970. And many famous colleges, including the Ivy Leagues, did not allow women to enroll. Women were not allowed to hold certain jobs and were harassed for wanting to join some companies. Because many universities (and high schools) took money from the federal government, the government could have a say in how the schools worked.

The Education Amendments Act basically said if a school wanted taxpayers' money, they had to make everything as equal as possible. The law made a huge difference in education. By 2022, more than 39 percent of American women had college degrees, and more than 60 percent of today's college students are women.

In this law, there was no direct mention of sports or athletics. But Title IX, the name of one section of that law, called for equal access to all school programs and activities. Over time, this would change women's sports for good.

Soon after the Education Amendments Act was signed, women around the country began pointing to Title IX to ask for better funding for women's sports. In the 1970s, one women's basketball team took to the court wearing white shirts with colored tape for numbers. They were highlighting the abysmal state of the female sports program's budgets: some were less than $1,000.

By the mid-1980s, most major sports had separate titles for women, but there were no national championships in college sports for women.

Over time, more and more money was dedicated to women's sports, more and more women got the chance to compete, and all that talent meant that more and more women had shots at pro sports too, either in the United States or overseas. Without Title IX, none of that would have happened.

But Title IX was not enough. We can look at the modern sports world and still find examples:

In 2019, after winning three Women's World Cups in soccer, the U.S. Women's National Team had to sue the national soccer federation to force them into paying the women's team as much as the men's team, which had never even made it into the quarterfinals at a World Cup. (In 2022, the women's team won the suit and signed a deal for equal pay!)

In 2021, women's college basketball players shocked their fans by showing, via online videos, the huge difference between the gyms and rooms that NCAA men's and women's basketball playoff teams were given. By the next tournament, things were much better—though still not equal.

As big a success as the WNBA has been, in 2022, the Los Angeles Sparks team had to sleep overnight at an airport after their flight was canceled. On the other hand, NBA teams fly charter airplanes, which means each flight is just theirs...no cancellations.

While there is clearly still work to be done, Title IX was more than just a first step. It allowed millions of girls and women the right to show their stuff on the fields, courts, diamonds, and rinks. It called for equality, and it is still calling.

JIM EISENREICH

First Major Leaguer with Tourette Syndrome

———

BORN 1959

When baseball player Jim Eisenreich was growing up in St. Cloud, Minnesota, he was teased for something he couldn't control. He was an amazing athlete, but his body often jerked uncontrollably with different tics. He couldn't stop blinking his eyes, and when he was nervous or uncomfortable, he would cough or clear his throat repeatedly. Kids and even teachers thought he was doing his tics on purpose and could stop if he wanted to do so. But Jim knew this wasn't the case.

"Teachers thought I had behavior problems," Jim explained. "They thought I just wanted attention."

Despite these challenges, Jim excelled in high school and college and was drafted by the Minnesota Twins. He could run down any fly ball in the field and smashed balls into the gaps between fielders when batting.

During Jim's rookie season with the Twins in 1982, he was off to a promising start. But after thirty-four games, his tics and jerks became so bad that he couldn't play anymore. The more Jim tried to stop, the worse the tics got.

Jim hardly played any baseball for the next four seasons. Finally, he rejoined the MLB in 1987 for the Kansas City Royals—and this is when his life changed. After years of doctor's appointments and testing, Jim was finally diagnosed with Tourette syndrome.

He was the first major-league player ever to be diagnosed with this condition. Tourette syndrome is when your brain makes your body move or say something that you don't want to do or say. Once Jim knew what he had, he was able to get the medical help he needed.

Jim played another twelve years in the majors and finished his career with 1,160 hits. He competed in two World Series and won one with the Florida Marlins. He was named the Kansas City Royals MVP in 1989.

Once Jim retired, he founded the Jim Eisenreich Foundation for Children with Tourette Syndrome. He now travels the country telling his story and hoping to inspire children just like him.

"After getting diagnosed myself, I learned that there was hope and light at the end of the tunnel," Jim said. "I want to show and tell kids who are like me—that yes, there is hope. Everything can be okay—even better than okay."

GEORGE EYSER

First Olympian with an Amputation

1870–1919

Gymnast George Eyser won six medals in one day at the 1904 Olympics, a record that still stands. Yet that isn't even the most amazing part of his story. George only had one leg, and he was the first athlete with an amputation to compete in the Olympic Games.

George was born in Germany. While growing up, he was run over by a train, and his left leg had to be amputated after the accident. He was fitted with a wooden prosthetic (an artificial leg) to help him walk, run, and even jump.

When George was fourteen years old, his family moved to St. Louis, Missouri, and George became a U.S. citizen. In St. Louis, George worked as a bookkeeper and joined a gymnastics club named Concordia Turnverein, which means "turning" in German. At this club, George discovered how good he was at the sport and how much passion he had for it.

The 1904 Olympics were held in George's hometown of St. Louis. This was the first Olympic Games that awarded gold, silver, and bronze medals. George won at least one of each! He captured gold in rope climbing, the vault, and parallel bars. He won silver medals in the pommel horse and in the overall competition. And he snagged a bronze medal in the high bar.

George relied on his upper-body strength when he competed. But when he did the vault, he had to jump off his right leg and his wooden leg, because there was no springboard back then to help him elevate.

The crowds loved George, and he loved competing. He continued competing after the Olympics as well: his club team won an international competition in 1908 and another national one in Ohio in 1909.

The first Paralympics (see page 68) were held in 1960—fifty-six years after George's amazing debut. While George is not the only athlete with an amputation to have competed in the traditional Olympic Games, he remains the first and only athlete with an amputation to ever win a medal—and he won six!

TOM FLORES

First Mexican American Super Bowl Coach

———

BORN 1937

Tom Flores was the head coach of the Oakland (now Las Vegas) Raiders when they won Super Bowl XV and again for Super Bowl XVIII. He was the first Mexican American coach to lead his team to victory, but these wins were not the first time Tom had broken barriers in the sport he loved.

Tom grew up in California's Central Valley, the son of Mexican immigrant parents who worked in the area's farms and vineyards. He loved football and was good enough to play at the University of the Pacific. While players with Hispanic backgrounds were not barred from playing in the pros, very few did, so Tom did not have role models who looked like him growing up. But that didn't stop him, and after being cut by two NFL teams, Tom joined the Oakland Raiders of the new American Football League in 1960. He earned the position of quarterback and started the first game in team history. In 1970, he won a Super Bowl ring as a backup quarterback with the Kansas City Chiefs.

After his playing career was over, Tom turned to coaching. Again, he found few Mexican Americans who had come before him. But Tom buckled down, worked hard, and became an assistant coach with the Raiders when they won Super Bowl XI. When John Madden retired in 1979, the Raiders made Tom only the second Hispanic head coach in league history.

Tom knew he had earned the job with talent, not as a token. "It doesn't matter what your color is, you have to be ready to perform and win, or you're going to be unemployed," he said later.

With Tom in charge, the Raiders won two more Super Bowls. He is one of only two people ever to win rings as a player, assistant coach, and head coach. Tom led the Raiders until 1989, when he broke another barrier: the Seattle Seahawks made him the NFL's first person of color to be named a team's president and general manager. He later coached the Seahawks as well, wrapping up his long NFL career in 1994 before turning to broadcasting.

Today, hundreds of football players and coaches point to Tom Flores as an inspiration in their lives and careers. His many achievements on and off the field were honored in 2021 when he was elected to the Pro Football Hall of Fame, joining fellow Mexican American NFL pioneer Tom Fears.

ALTHEA GIBSON

First Black Grand Slam Champion in Tennis

———

1927–2003

Few athletes have traveled a more complicated road to international stardom than Althea Gibson, who went from poverty in the streets of Harlem to the top of the world of tennis. Her talent and tenacity made her a barrier-breaking champion.

Althea was born in South Carolina but grew up in Harlem, New York. She was a great athlete as a kid, quickly taking to tennis after becoming a city paddle tennis champion when she was twelve. Supported by Black businesspeople and tennis fans, Althea slowly improved her game. By 1947, she was a national champion in the American Tennis Association, an all-Black series created because Black players were banned from other tournaments. Althea would go on to win ten straight ATA titles. But she and her supporters wanted more.

After Jackie Robinson's debut in baseball in 1947, pressure grew to let Althea take part in the U.S. National Championships, the tournament that later became the U.S. Open. Still, she was turned down because of her race. In 1950, she was finally invited, partially thanks to Grand Slam champion Alice Marble, a white athlete who called out the racism in the tennis community. (A Grand Slam title is earned at one of the four major tournaments: Wimbledon, the French Open, the U.S. Open, and the Australian Open.)

Althea used that as a springboard to a great career. In 1956, she became the first Black athlete to win the French Open, one of tennis's Grand Slam events. The next year, she became the first Black player to win at England's Wimbledon, the oldest and most famous tournament in the world. She won the doubles title but lost in the singles quarterfinals.

Althea returned to Wimbledon in 1957, where she won the ladies' singles title and was presented with her prize by Queen Elizabeth II. "Shaking hands with the Queen was a long way from being forced to sit in the colored section of the bus [when I visited] Wilmington, North Carolina," Althea said later. New York City welcomed Althea home with a ticker-tape parade down Broadway. That September, also in New York City, she won the U.S. National Championships. She was the first Black person to win there, cementing her position as the world's number one women's player.

Althea retired from amateur tennis in 1958 so she could play in pro events. In 1964, she also became the first Black player on the Ladies Professional Golf Association (LPGA) tour. Althea's success in tennis blazed a trail for many others to follow, including Arthur Ashe, the first Black man to repeat her feats as the U.S. Open (1968) and Wimbledon (1975) champion.

JANET GUTHRIE

First Woman to Race the Indy 500

———

BORN 1938

In 1977, Janet Guthrie became the first woman to race in the Indianapolis 500. But fans and the other racers—all men—did not think she belonged there. They criticized her and called her names. Fellow drivers said, "She should be home having babies." But Janet was smart and brave enough not to listen. She knew she belonged on the track.

"Racing is one of the few sports in which women can compete on an equal basis," she said. "It is a matter of a spirit, really."

Janet had been born with this daring spirit. Her father was an airline pilot, and Janet earned a pilot's license when she was seventeen years old. In college, she studied physics and might have become a pilot herself, but women were not allowed to fly commercial planes or military planes at the time. So instead, she decided to try car racing.

"The bug bit me hard and deep," Janet said. "Car racing took over my life."

Before Indianapolis, Janet had been a pro driver for thirteen years, racing on the Sports Car Club of America circuit and winning several major races. She even built her own car engines for some of the races. But the Indy 500 is a big deal. It is called the Super Bowl of car racing because it is the sport's most important and popular event. Cars whip around a track at speeds topping 200 miles per hour.

In Janet's first attempt to race the Indy 500, at thirty-eight years old, she did not complete the race because her car had mechanical issues. But the following year, she was back in Indianapolis again. She crossed the finish line in ninth place in a field of thirty-three drivers. And she drove the entire race with a broken wrist!

When Janet retired in 1983, she had competed in eleven IndyCar events in her career and thirty-three NASCAR Cup races in five seasons. NASCAR races are done with stock cars, which are a lot heavier and bigger than Indy cars. Janet's highest finish of sixth place in a NASCAR race remains tied as the best finish ever by a female driver.

But more important than her records, Janet proved that women could compete with men. Thanks to her, other female drivers followed in her footsteps or, rather, in her treads.

BECKY HAMMON

First Woman to Coach an NBA Team

BORN 1977

Since basketball was invented in 1891, men have coached women's basketball in high school, college, and the pros. Women have coached women too, but they never coached men—at least not in the pros. That is, until Becky Hammon. In 2020, Becky became the first woman to be a head coach (for one game) in the NBA.

Becky Hammon grew up in South Dakota and played hoops at Colorado State. In 1999, she joined the New York Liberty of the WNBA, where she played for several years.

In 2007, she moved to the San Antonio Silver Stars, which later became the Las Vegas Aces, for the second half of her great sixteen-year career. Becky was a six-time all-star, played in four WNBA finals, and retired in the top 10 of WNBA scoring. In 2023, Becky was elected to the Basketball Hall of Fame for her great playing career.

A knee injury in 2013 marked the end of Becky's playing career, but she knew she wanted to try coaching. Fortunately, the same people who owned the Silver Stars also owned the NBA's San Antonio Spurs. While Becky rehabbed her knee, she unofficially shadowed the Spurs' coaches during the 2013–2014 NBA season. After she officially retired as a player, the Spurs hired her in 2014 as the first full-time female assistant coach in NBA history! Becky quickly proved she could coach as well as she could play.

Becky became the head coach of the Spurs' NBA Summer League team and led them to a championship. She also helped with the 2016 NBA All-Star team under head coach Gregg Popovich. In 2020, Becky became the senior assistant coach, and another barrier-breaking moment came on December 30, 2020, when Spurs head coach Gregg Popovich was ejected from a game against the Los Angeles Lakers, and Becky stepped in.

She said after the game, "He officially pointed at me. That was it. [He] said, 'You've got them.' Obviously, it's a big deal. It's a substantial moment." Becky became the first woman to be in charge of an NBA team during a game.

Becky has opened a lot of doors. As many as fifteen women have earned NBA coaching staff positions since 2014. For her part, Becky wanted to lead a team full-time, and in 2022, she returned to the WNBA to take over as head coach of the Las Vegas Aces, where she was named the league's Coach of the Year. And who knows? The NBA might call again.

ERIN JACKSON

First Black Female Individual Gold Medalist in the Winter Olympics

—

BORN 1992

Speed skater Erin Jackson was the first Black woman to win a gold medal in an individual event at the Winter Olympics when she secured the gold in the 500-meter speed skating race at the 2022 Games in Beijing.

Growing up in Florida, Erin described herself as a "rink rat." But not an ice-skating rink rat. "I spent my days at roller rinks skating around with my friends and listening to music, eating pizza at the snack bar," Erin said with a smile.

Sometimes Erin got into trouble for skating too fast at the roller rink. So she started competing in inline skating, where speed wasn't only allowed, it was encouraged. She was named the U.S. Olympic Committee Female Athlete of the Year for Roller Sports in 2012 and 2013. But she kept thinking about one thing: inline skating was not actually a sport in the Olympic Games.

Erin went to college at the University of Florida, but after college, she still had the Olympic dream. Erin moved to Salt Lake City, Utah, and switched to speed skating on ice in 2017. After only four months in the new sport, she qualified for the 2018 Winter Olympics and finished in 24th place. But reaching the Olympics wasn't enough for her. Erin wanted to be an Olympic medal winner!

She started preparing for the next games right away, but her dreams were almost derailed at the trials. She slipped in the 500 meters and barely missed one of the qualifying spots. Her good friend Brittany Bowe, who had qualified for the Games in other speed skating races, gave up her spot in the 500 so Erin could race.

"There was no one more deserving than Erin," Brittany said about giving the spot to her friend.

At the 2022 Games, Erin proved her friend right. She won the gold medal by .08 seconds. In addition to being the first Black woman to win gold in speed skating, Erin was the first woman from the United States of any race to win a speed skating gold in twenty years. And she is not done yet: Erin plans to keep competing.

"It would be awesome if I wasn't the first and there were plenty of people before me," Erin said about her role as a Black woman in speed skating. "But since I'm the first, I hope I set a good path and inspire more people like me to get out there and try these winter sports."

JACK JOHNSON

First Black World Heavyweight Boxing Champion

1878–1946

In the early 1900s, whoever held the title of world heavyweight boxing champion was automatically one of the most famous people in the world. Until 1908, all those people were white. Jack Johnson changed that and, in some ways, changed America.

Jack was born in Galveston in 1878, the son of formerly enslaved people. He began boxing when he was nineteen years old and won fight after fight—but almost always against Black opponents. The idea that a Black man could hit a white man, let alone beat him in a match, was shocking at the time. Black people throughout America faced discrimination of all sorts, and boxers were no different.

Jack became one of the top boxers in the country, but because he was Black, he was not allowed a shot at the heavyweight title. In 1905, Canadian Tommy Burns claimed the title, and Jack began his pursuit of a match— literally. Tommy fought in the United States, England, and France, and Jack followed him wherever he went, a bold move for a Black man at the time. Finally, in 1908, Tommy agreed to fight Jack. In fourteen brutal rounds, Jack won and became the first Black world heavyweight champ.

For the next seven years, the boxing world tried to take away Jack's title. In fact, some boxers were called "the Great White Hope" as they attempted to defeat him. In 1910, former champ Jim Jeffries came out of retirement to take on Jack. "I am going into this fight for the purpose of proving that a white man is better than a Negro," he boasted. In one of boxing's most famous bouts, Jack beat Jeffries.

Jack lived his life the way he wanted, ignoring what the white community thought a Black man should act like. Then in 1913, Jack was convicted of breaking the Mann Act, a racist law that banned Black men from "transporting" white women across state lines. (Jack had driven with his future wife, Lucille Cameron, from Wisconsin to Illinois.) Rather than go to jail, Jack left the United States. He fought overseas for seven years, defeating every challenger before losing the title in 1915 to Jess Willard in Cuba. In 1920, Jack returned to serve his prison sentence and continued boxing until 1928. He was finally pardoned of his crime long after his death, in 2018.

Jack Johnson's power, talent, and style made him a world hero. American racism fought back with anger and the law, but Jack never backed down, and he remains a trail-blazing hero to millions.

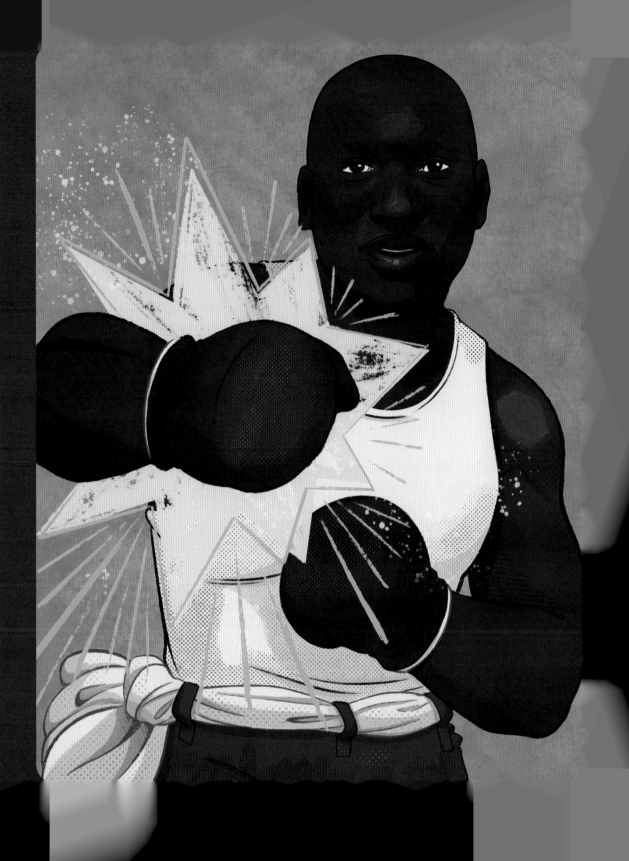

JULIE KRONE

First Female Jockey to Win a Triple Crown Race

BORN 1963

Many little girls love horses, yet only a few get the chance to ride them. Even fewer get to call themselves jockeys—and then there is Julie Krone.

On June 5, 1993, Julie became the first and only (so far) woman to win a Triple Crown race. The three Triple Crown races are the most important in horse racing and include the Kentucky Derby, the Preakness Stakes in Maryland, and the Belmont Stakes in New York. Julie rode a horse named Colonial Affair to win the Belmont, which is the oldest and longest race of the three.

"I was so spunky in my approach," Julie said about her riding. "I was absolutely relentless. The biggest compliment I received was that I was an awesome jockey. Not an awesome *female* jockey—just an awesome jockey."

Julie grew up on a horse farm in Michigan. When she was fourteen years old, she watched a professional horse race on television and knew right then that she wanted to be a jockey too. She rode in her first race when she was eighteen years old and won one a month later. Julie was a brave rider. Jockeys are all small, but Julie was even small by those standards. Standing at four feet, ten inches tall and weighing only one hundred pounds, she rode horses that weighed over one thousand pounds. Yet she commanded them with strength and finesse.

Two months after her Belmont victory, Julie suffered a terrible fall off her horse and shattered her ankle. She spent nine months in rehabilitation. Just weeks after her return, Julie fell again, breaking her wrist and finger. Because of these injuries, Julie began to suffer from depression and anxiety. She was so afraid of falling again and did not want to ride anymore. A doctor diagnosed Julie with post-traumatic stress disorder (PTSD), a mental health condition that occurs after a scary or difficult event. Thankfully, her doctor helped Julie regain the confidence and joy to race again.

Julie recovered to win more than 3,700 races in her twenty-two-year career—the most by any woman to date. In 2000, she became the first woman to be inducted into the horse racing Hall of Fame, and she retired in 2003.

Julie was honored by the Women's Sports Foundation in 2004 with the Wilma Rudolph Courage Award. The award was given to Julie because, after every fall and setback, she got back up and rode. Is there any better message for an athlete and a person?

JEREMY LIN

First Taiwanese American NBA Star

BORN 1988

In February 2012, Jeremy Lin had rarely played in the NBA before breaking out with a string of amazing games. The player from California, whose parents were from Taiwan, became an overnight sensation and an inspiration to other Asian American athletes.

NBA players from Asian countries, such as China's Yao Ming, had previously become NBA stars. But Asian Americans were a real rarity in the sport. Very few played high school or college ball, and therefore, none headed to the NBA. In fact, before Jeremy, the only previous Asian American NBA player was Wat Misaka, a Japanese American, who played three games more than fifty years prior, in 1947.

So when Lin poured in 25 points in a New York Knicks win and followed that with eight more 20-plus-point games in the next few weeks, people called it "Linsanity." Jeremy was called "Lincredible!"

Sadly, he also faced some racist remarks. The NBA was new to Jeremy, but being treated differently because of his background was not. Others had been saying nasty things about his Asian identity since he was in high school. Even as he was leading his high school team to the state championship, and Harvard University to the Ivy League title, he endured insults.

But Jeremy didn't let that—or anything—stop him. After signing as a free agent with the Golden State Warriors, he moved to the Knicks in late 2011. About a month later, his life changed forever with Linsanity. Unfortunately, Jeremy was injured in late March and missed the rest of that season. He went on to play seven more NBA seasons with six teams. In 2019, while with the Toronto Raptors, Jeremy became the first Asian American to win an NBA championship. He also played several years for pro teams in China.

At first, Jeremy struggled in his role as an Asian American sports pioneer. As he matured, he proudly accepted the role and became a bigger advocate for Asian American athletes. In 2021, he tweeted, "To the next generation of Asian American ballers—when you get your shot, do NOT hesitate. Don't worry whether anyone else thinks you belong. When you get your foot in the door, KICK THAT DOOR OPEN. And then bring others with you." That's what Jeremy sure did, and he will be an NBA legend forever.

A Groundbreaking Game: TEXAS WESTERN MINERS

Before the 1966 NCAA men's basketball championship, Adolph Rupp, the legendary University of Kentucky men's basketball head coach, said, "No five Black players are going to beat Kentucky." Rupp, who'd won four NCAA titles and led the nation's top-ranked team into the final, refused to recruit Black players for his own team.

Facing Rupp's Wildcats were the Texas Western Miners—a team with an all-Black starting lineup. Not one player on the Miners was an all-star, and nobody had been awarded an individual award. But once the Texas Western players heard what Rupp said, they were determined more than ever to win. One Miner starting player, forward Harry Flournoy, declared he knew that Kentucky had as much a chance now of winning as a snowball surviving in hell.

The Miners played suffocating defense against the Wildcats, stealing passes right and left. They were lightning quick—three speedy guards were starters—and outran the Wildcats up and down the court. Guard Bobby Joe Hill led the scoring charge, finishing the game with twenty points. The Miners took the lead midway through the first half and never looked back. They hit their mid-range jumpers and made twenty-six out of twenty-seven foul shots in one stretch. The final score was 72–65.

Most importantly, this game was nationally televised, which was rare at the time. The Miners' victory was con-sidered a giant upset and became a huge deal to the Black communities watching the game from home. An all-Black starting lineup had defeated an all-white Kentucky team! This was the first time this had ever happened in a national title game. The game also took place during the civil rights movement, when there was a lot of social unrest in the United States. As a result, the victory was about more than just basketball.

"Kentucky was playing for a commemorative wristwatch and the right to say they were national champions," said Flournoy. "We were out to prove that it didn't matter what color a person's skin was."

At the time of the game, there were no Black basketball players in any school in the Southwestern Conference, the Southeastern Conference (Kentucky's conference), and the Atlantic Coast Conference—essentially all the colleges and universities in the South. So this game was a major step toward integration in college sports, as schools all over the country began to recruit Black athletes for all their sports teams, not just basketball.

However, this change didn't come easily. Texas Western's coach, Don Haskins, a white man, received forty thousand pieces of hate mail after his team's victory. He even received death threats. But Haskins never doubted his decision. "You guys got a lot of Black kids to earn scholarships around this country," Haskins told his championship team years later. "You can be proud of that. I guess you helped change the world a little bit."

Forty years after their victory, the Miners were inducted into the Naismith Memorial Basketball Hall of Fame. That same year, they visited the White House and were honored at the halftime of the NCAA championship game. They joined the National Collegiate Basketball Hall of Fame in 2020. At the ceremony, the players were called "pioneering roundballers" who changed college basketball forever.

NANCY LOPEZ

First Hispanic LPGA Champion

BORN 1957

As a Mexican American female golfer growing up in the 1960s, Nancy had very few role models, since most American golfers played at fancy country clubs, many of which excluded people of color. But Nancy did have her father, Domingo, who taught her to play golf. At first, the only clubs she had were her dad's cut down to size, but she still took to the game quickly.

By the time Nancy was twelve years old, she was the state amateur champion, and she later became the two-time U.S. Juniors champ. In 1977, she was the first Hispanic golfer to join the LPGA Tour. A year later, Nancy stunned the golf world by winning nine tournaments, five of which she won in a row—an LPGA record. Nancy was the Rookie of the Year, received the Vare Trophy for lowest scoring average, and was Player of the Year. No other female golfer has ever matched that triple play. Nancy's success made her nationally famous, and the Associated Press awarded her Female Athlete of the Year, a rare honor for a golfer.

In 1979, Nancy won eight more tournaments and earned Player of the Year again. After her amazing start, Nancy continued as one of the best golfers in the world for more than twenty-five years, securing forty-eight career wins on the LPGA Tour and receiving Player of the Year twice more, in 1985 and 1988. In 2007, the LPGA created an award for leadership and service in her honor. Nancy was also inducted into the World Golf and LPGA Halls of Fame. The little girl from New Mexico had come a long way.

Nancy retired from golf in 2008 but remains involved in her golf equipment company and charity work. In 2013, a panel of sports experts voted Nancy the most influential Hispanic athlete of all time. Nancy is proud of her heritage, and she recognizes the impact she has had.

"I think I opened a lot of doors for many people of color, not just Hispanics," she said. Indeed, thanks in part to Nancy's trailblazing work, the LPGA now includes players from many backgrounds and more than a dozen countries. It's not an all-white sport anymore.

CLAY MARZO

First Autism Advocate in Professional Surfing

BORN 1989

Surfer Clay Marzo is most at home in the water. Clay grew up in Maui, Hawaii, and was surfing almost as soon as he could walk. He would spend six to eight hours a day in the water, and by age fifteen, Clay had won a national title in surfing. Clay can do things on his board that nobody else can do. No matter how big the wave, Clay can usually stay up on the board. He contorts his body in ways no other surfer can, almost like his entire body is double-jointed.

"Clay is a freak on the surfboard," said nine-time world champion Kelly Slater. "He does things people don't even think of. He just sees the wave his own way."

But when Clay was growing up outside the water, he was lost. "Life out of the water for Clay does not come easy," said his mom, Jill Marzo. "When he's not in the ocean, he becomes uncomfortable in his own skin."

In school, Clay had trouble sitting still. He struggled with following directions. He had difficulty reading people's facial expressions. Clay would sometimes blurt out direct and unkind words. As a result, Clay did not make friends easily, and people called him weird and strange.

In 2007, when Clay was eighteen years old, he was diagnosed as being on the autism spectrum. Being on the autism spectrum affects the brain, making it difficult for those who are on it to make eye contact and interact with others. They also tend to be laser-focused on one thing and can get upset when their routine is altered. Once Clay was diagnosed, he and his family were relieved. They understood the reason Clay behaved the way he did.

Clay became one of the first professional athletes to openly talk about his condition, and thankfully, he didn't see it as something that needed to be fixed.

"It's a gift," Clay said. "With surfing, with the way I see the world, with everything."

Once diagnosed, Clay attended therapy sessions to help him fit in better on land. The sessions taught him how to understand people and stay calm in group situations. Clay began volunteering with a group called Surfers Healing. The organization works with kids with autism and teaches them how to surf.

Clay remains one of the best and most unique surfers in the world. And the fact that he is on the autism spectrum is a part of all of this.

KYLE MAYNARD

First Quadruple Amputee Professional Athlete

———

BORN 1986

Here is a list of Kyle Maynard's accomplishments: He won thirty-five wrestling matches as a high school senior in Georgia. He ascended to the summit of Mount Aconcagua (22,838 feet), the highest peak in the Americas. He climbed Mount Kilimanjaro (19,341 feet), the world's sixth tallest mountain. He wrote a bestselling autobiography, *No Excuses*, and opened his own CrossFit gym. He is a competitive weight lifter and has fought in the sport of mixed martial arts. Kyle is also the first quadruple amputee to do all these things.

"When people meet Kyle, they are humbled," explained Kyle's high school wrestling coach Cliff Ramos. "They are changed."

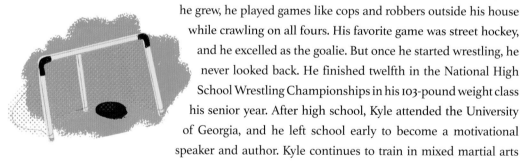

Kyle was born with a condition called congenital amputation. He has arms that end at the elbows, and he has legs that end at the knees. He does not use prosthetics of any kind in his daily life, when he competes, or even when he climbs to the top of mountains. He crawls on all fours.

"I am as fierce a competitor on the inside as anyone can be," Kyle wrote in his book. "On my shoulder is a tattoo of a tiger; that's how I think of myself, and that's how I fight."

When Kyle was born, his mom and dad wondered what kind of life their son would lead. They did not know if he could live a fulfilling life, but Kyle figured it out right away! As he grew, he played games like cops and robbers outside his house while crawling on all fours. His favorite game was street hockey, and he excelled as the goalie. But once he started wrestling, he never looked back. He finished twelfth in the National High School Wrestling Championships in his 103-pound weight class his senior year. After high school, Kyle attended the University of Georgia, and he left school early to become a motivational speaker and author. Kyle continues to train in mixed martial arts and weightlifting, and he won the ESPY Award for best athlete with a disability twice.

Whenever Kyle speaks, the audience and location change, but his message does not. "The root of the message is the same: it is no excuses," explained Kyle. "If you want something bad enough, you go out there and fight for it. People are stronger for what they face."

BILLY MILLS

First American to Win Olympic 10,000-Meter Race

———

BORN 1938

When Billy Mills stepped up to the starting line of the 10,000-meter race at the 1964 Olympic Games in Tokyo, hardly anybody knew who he was. One announcer called Billy an overlooked underdog.

But Billy had been dreaming about winning this race for a long time. He had been training as hard as he could leading up to the day, and during the race, Billy surprised the other runners by staying with the leaders. In the final lap, Ron Clarke and Mohammed Gammoudi jostled Billy as they raced for the finish line. But in the final thirty meters, Billy sprinted past both and won the race by less than three yards!

Billy had pulled off one of the biggest upsets in Olympic history. His winning time of 28:24.4, which was a new Olympic record, was almost fifty seconds faster than even he had ever run. Billy became the first (and only) American to win the gold medal in this event.

Billy grew up on the Pine Ridge Indian Reservation in South Dakota. He is Oglala Lakota. The reservation did not have plumbing or paved highways, and many families lacked necessary resources. "I never even owned a pair of shoes of my own until the night before the Olympic Games," Billy said.

Billy and his family faced racism because of their Indigenous heritage. They were refused service in restaurants and called names. Billy's mother and father both died by the time he was twelve years old. After that, Billy was sent to live at a boarding school in Lawrence, Kansas, where he discovered his love for running. When he graduated, he joined the track team at the University of Kansas for two years but later quit college because of the racist insults he faced.

"It broke me inside," Billy said about that time. But when he remembered the words that his father spoke to him, "You need a dream to heal a broken soul," he started running again. "I healed my broken soul," Billy said after winning the Olympic gold.

Billy wanted to help heal other broken souls too. After his running career, he cofounded the organization Running Strong for American Indian Youth, which helps kids like Billy achieve their dreams. In 2012, President Obama awarded Billy the Presidential Citizens Medal. The announcer said about Billy at the ceremony, "The United States honors Billy Mills for inspiring young people to find the best in themselves."

IBTIHAJ MUHAMMAD

First Muslim American Olympic Medalist to Wear a Hijab

BORN 1985

Growing up in Maplewood, New Jersey, Olympic bronze-medal-winning fencer Ibtihaj Muhammad played all kinds of sports. Her father taught her how to throw and catch, play basketball, and swim. In addition to being athletic, Ibtihaj's family members are also devout Muslims. They observe the Islamic practice of hijab.

"Hijab literally means 'to cover' in Arabic," explained Ibtihaj. "Women who observe hijab cover everything with the exception of the face and their hands."

Ibtihaj was part of the basketball and volleyball teams in grade school, and she was the only one on either squad who observed hijab while playing.

"I always felt like there was a barrier between me and my teammates because I never looked like them," Ibtihaj explained.

Then when Ibtihaj was twelve, she and her mom spotted fencers practicing at a local high school. Ibtihaj noticed that those athletes competed beneath a bodysuit as well as a full mask to protect themselves from their opponent's sword.

"I knew I would not have to change a part of who I was in order to fit in with the sport," Ibtihaj explained. So she tried it out.

Ibtihaj discovered she was a natural fencer, and she excelled at saber. She led her high school to two state championship titles, attended Duke University, and was a three-time All-American there.

After graduating, Ibtihaj continued training and became a member of the U.S. National fencing team in 2010. Then at the 2016 Olympics in Rio de Janeiro, Ibtihaj won a bronze medal in the team sabre event. She became the first Muslim American woman to compete and win a medal for the United States in the Olympics while wearing a headscarf.

Despite her success, Ibtihaj faced prejudice and even death threats from strangers because she observed hijab. This made Ibtihaj want to speak out about her faith even more. She serves as an ambassador for the Empowering Women and Girls Through Sports Initiative and speaks to audiences all around the world. She founded a clothing company that brings modest and affordable clothes to the United States, and has written a memoir and two children's books about the Muslim American experience.

"It's important to me that youth everywhere, no matter their race, religion, or gender, know that anything is possible with perseverance," she said.

SHIRLEY MULDOWNEY

First Female Drag Racing Champion

BORN 1940

Few sports have historically been as male dominated as drag racing. Just about every motorsport, in fact, had been closed off to female drivers since...well, since car racing began in the late 1800s. But from the time she was a young girl growing up in upstate New York, Shirley Muldowney loved speed and was determined to race.

But even as she won street race after street race, Shirley could not crack into the official ranks of professional drag racers. In this high-speed sport, drivers steer specialized cars called dragsters down quarter-mile tracks, sometimes topping 300 miles per hour in races that last only a few seconds. It's a sport that takes skill, timing, and courage.

Shirley was almost twenty-five years old before she was given a license to join the National Hot Rod Association (NHRA), only the second woman to earn one. As she began her pro career driving the Funny Car style of a dragster, she was jeered by fans and insulted by fellow drivers. But Shirley just kept driving...fast.

Soon after winning her first Funny Car event in 1971, she was the first woman allowed to move up to Top Fuel, the fastest and most famous type of drag racing. Five years later, Shirley was voted Driver of the Year. And in 1977, she notched her most famous first: she won the Top Fuel title, which made her the first woman to be the national champion of any major motorsports series.

Known by her nickname "Cha Cha" and for her hot-pink Top Fuel dragster, Shirley kept driving and winning. In 1982, she won Top Fuel for the third time. Not only was she the first woman to do so, but she was the first NHRA driver ever—male or female—with three season titles.

Shirley became an inspiration to women and a national sports celebrity. A movie about Shirley's life, *Heart Like a Wheel*, was released in 1983. But the next year, she suffered a terrible wreck and was badly injured. Still, Shirley fought to get better as she had fought to make her mark, and she returned to the track to win again.

Since Shirley's retirement in 2003, other women have gone on to win national championships in the Pro Stock (Erica Enders) and Pro Stock Motorcycle (Angelle Sampey) categories. But Shirley will always have been the first to cross that finish line.

NBA TRIO

First Black Players in the NBA

COOPER: 1926–1984, LLOYD: 1928–2015, CLIFTON: 1922–1990

Today, players from more than a dozen countries are in the NBA, and about 75 percent of the league's players are Black. Knowing this, it's shocking that pro hoops was thirteen years old before the first African Americans were allowed to play.

Black people had played basketball for years, of course, and traveling teams like the Harlem Rens had won national championships playing against all-white teams. The National Basketball League (NBL) started in 1937, and the rival Basketball Association of America (BAA) began in 1946. But neither of these included Black players.

Then two important things happened. In 1947, Jackie Robinson started playing Major League Baseball. Then in 1949, the NBL and BAA merged to form the National Basketball Association (NBA). After its first season, it became clear the NBA had to end its racist practices.

During the 1950 NBA draft, the Boston Celtics made Chuck Cooper the first Black player drafted. Later in that same draft, the Washington Capitols selected Earl Lloyd, and the New York Knicks picked Nat "Sweetwater" Clifton. (An all-around athlete and army veteran, Nat had been a star for the Harlem Globetrotters and played baseball in the Negro Leagues.)

On October 31, 1950, Earl became the first Black player in an NBA game. The next night, Chuck made his debut for Boston. Three days later, Nat took the court for the Knicks.

These pioneering players all had solid NBA careers for several teams. Earl became the first Black player on a championship team in 1955 with the Syracuse Nationals and was later the NBA's second Black head coach, after Boston's Bill Russell in 1966. Chuck played six seasons, and Nat helped the Knicks reach three finals during his eight seasons. All three players were later elected to the Naismith Memorial Basketball Hall of Fame.

And here's to Harold Hunter! He was drafted in the tenth round of the 1950 NBA Draft and was *officially* the first to sign a contract with an NBA team. However, he was cut by the Washington Capitols before ever appearing in a game. He later became a high school and college basketball coach.

The NBA and WNBA can both look back at Chuck, Earl, and Nat, and thank them for the incredible national and international success of basketball today.

NAT CLIFTON

EARL LLOYD

CHUCK COOPER

NEW YO
8

AASHING
15

BOSTO
11

NFL'S FORGOTTEN FOUR

First Black Players in the Modern NFL

WASHINGTON 1918–1971; STRODE 1914–1994; WILLIS 1921–2007; MOTLEY 1920–1999

When the NFL began in 1920, several Black players were on team rosters, including Fritz Pollard, who was also the coach of the Akron Pros in 1921. By the end of the decade, though, Black athletes were being kept out of the league. In 1933, a group of racist team owners even put together an unofficial ban against Black players. Thankfully, after World War II ended in 1945, the tides began to turn.

It started in Los Angeles. The city group that ran the Coliseum, home of the NFL's Los Angeles Rams, was inspired by a local sportswriter and input from the Black community. The group declared the Rams could not play there until they signed a Black player.

Across town, Kenny Washington had been a star at UCLA before the war. He had graduated several years earlier and was working as a Los Angeles police officer. He put

down his badge when the Rams added him to their roster, and became the first Black player signed to an NFL contract. Before the season began, Woody Strode also joined the team. Woody had a one-season NFL career before becoming an actor and stuntman, while Kenny played three seasons and was later elected to the Pro Football Hall of Fame. These two were officially the first Black players in the modern NFL.

In the same year, the Cleveland Browns started in a rival league to the NFL, the All-America Football Conference (AAFC). Head coach Paul Brown had worked with Black athletes on military teams and knew there was no reason they should not join his new pro team. He signed lineman Bill Willis and running back Marion Motley to the Browns. Bill became one of the greatest blockers in NFL history, a fierce and powerful player who often had to ignore racist taunts from opponents. Marion was one of the finest runners ever, knowing that he would be tackled extra hard by racist opponents but pounding through them anyway. Together, the pair helped the Browns win all four AAFC titles, plus one NFL title after the two leagues merged in 1950. Both players were easy choices for the Pro Football Hall of Fame as well.

In honor of their pioneering play, a year before Jackie Robinson broke baseball's color barrier, the "Forgotten Four" were given the Ralph Hay Pioneer Award by the NFL in 2022.

MARION
MOTLEY

WOODY
STRODE

BILL
WILLIS

KENNY
WASHINGTON

KIM NG

First Female MLB General Manager

—

BORN 1968

A baseball "lifer," Kim Ng didn't want any favors or special treatment. She just wanted a chance. After more than thirty years of working her way up the ranks, she got that chance...and made history. In 2022, Kim was named the first female general manager (GM) of a Major League Baseball team. In fact, she was the first woman to hold that key job in any of the biggest North American men's sports leagues (NFL, NBA, MLB, NHL).

Kim grew up in New York and New Jersey, where she played softball and learned to love baseball with her dad, who was of Chinese descent. Kim's mom had a Thai and Chinese background. Kim played softball at the University of Chicago and then set her sights on a job in the major leagues. In 1990, she got an unpaid internship with the Chicago White Sox and slowly moved up the ranks. Kim learned how baseball teams are built, how players are scouted, and how a sports organization works. In 1998, she was hired as an assistant general manager of the New York Yankees. Kim was the first woman—and one of the youngest ever—to have that title in baseball.

From 2002 to 2011, Kim was an assistant general manager for the Los Angeles Dodgers. Kim still had her eye on the top GM job, and she got used to being interviewed for open positions. Even though she knew some of the interviews were only to make the team look good for talking to a candidate of color, she kept going. Kim met with team after team—including the San Diego Padres, Seattle Mariners, and San Francisco Giants—about becoming their GM. But those teams always chose a man. "It's pretty crushing when you get turned down," Kim said. "To put myself through that was not always fun. But I thought it was necessary."

From 2011 to 2020, she worked for the office of the MLB commissioner as the senior vice president of baseball operations, helping to run the league's international division.

Finally, in November 2020, Kim got her dream job. Derek Jeter, the Hall of Fame former Yankees shortstop who had become the president of the Miami Marlins, hired her as the team's GM. Kim stayed with the Marlins through 2023, the year her team made the playoffs for the first time in twenty seasons. Women in sports everywhere—as well as Asian Americans—celebrated Kim's success. It took her thirty years to become a MLB GM, but thanks to Kim, hopefully it won't be thirty more years until another woman follows in her footsteps.

WILLIE O'REE

First Black Player in the NHL

———

BORN 1935

Throughout his playing days, Willie was called "the Jackie Robinson of hockey." Jackie was the first Black player in Major League Baseball and although Willie admired Jackie greatly, he made it clear he did not necessarily want that nickname.

"I am the Willie O'Ree of hockey," he said with a smile.

On January 18, 1958, Willie became the first Black player to compete in the NHL. He made his debut with the Boston Bruins. Breaking the color barrier for Willie was not as smooth as ice though. Sometimes fans spit on him, and he faced constant racism.

"Every game I played, there were racial remarks made toward me," Willie said. "They would say the N-word. They would say to me, 'What are you doing in a white man's game?' I just went over and played."

Willie grew up in Fredericton, New Brunswick, in Canada. He spent his childhood playing street hockey and ice hockey. After high school, he joined the minor hockey league in Quebec, Canada. He was a superfast winger who could beat most opponents to the puck. While in Quebec, the Bruins called and asked him to play for them.

Willie played in forty-six games with the Bruins between 1958 and 1961. His entire playing career spanned more than twenty-nine years, from 1950 to 1979, where he played mostly in the Western Hockey League.

Years after his career was over, the NHL reached out to Willie and asked him to become the director of youth services for its diversity task force. Willie began promoting the sport by holding clinics for children with diverse backgrounds. "When I talk to these children," Willie explained, "I tell them names will never hurt you unless you let them. Just play hockey."

The task force holds a Willie O'Ree All-Star game every year for ten- to twelve-year-old boys and girls that celebrates inclusion in the sport. The message of the diversity team is "Hockey is for everyone."

"Breaking into the NHL was great," Willie said. "But the work I do with these kids has to be the most rewarding work I have ever done."

Willie was inducted into the Hockey Hall of Fame in 2018, and the Bruins retired his No. 22 jersey in 2022. Since Willie first played in the NHL, more than one hundred players of color have followed.

A Movement of Inclusivity: PARALYMPICS

The Paralympics are sports competitions among athletes with disabilities from around the world. The word *paralympic* comes from the Greek word *para*, which means "alongside," combined with *Olympics* to give the meaning of two competitions that exist side by side. The first official Paralympic Games took place in Rome, Italy, in 1960, six days after the Olympics ended. Four hundred athletes from twenty-three different countries competed in eight different events that year. The Paralympics always take place in the same city where the Olympics are held. Paralympic athletes include amputees and athletes with cerebral palsy, intellectual disabilities, vision loss, and more.

Like the Olympics, the Paralympics alternate every two years between the Winter and Summer Games. And the Paralympians compete in many of the same events that the Olympians do, such as skiing in the Winter Games, and track and field events in the Summer Games. But the Paralympians have modified sports equipment and different playing rules in many cases.

"Paralympians smash stereotypes and demonstrate why persons with disabilities need to be active, visible, and contributing members of a global society," International Paralympic Committee president Andrew Parsons said.

The Paralympics began at a spinal injury center in the United Kingdom. The patients there were in wheelchairs and paralyzed from injuries suffered during World War II. A German-British doctor named Ludwig Guttmann wanted to teach these veterans how to lead independent and meaningful lives. So in 1948, to coincide with the Olympics in London, Dr. Guttmann held an archery contest among his patients. He then continued to hold a contest every four years at the same time as the Olympic Games. Competitors with similar disabilities from other countries joined the competition too. A sports movement was truly born.

"We not only saved the lives of these paraplegic or quadriplegic men, women, and children, but also gave them back their dignity, and made them happy and respected citizens," Dr. Guttmann said.

The motto of the Paralympics is "Spirit in motion." This means all the athletes who compete are always moving forward and never giving up, despite the difficulties they may face.

American swimmer Jessica Long is one of many Paralympians who embody this spirit. When Jessica was a baby, she was adopted from a Russian orphanage by an American family. When she was eighteen months old, Jessica had to have her legs amputated above her knees because she had been born without both fibula bones. As a result, she couldn't do all the things other children could do. But she could swim. She loved playing in her grandparents' pool.

"When I'm in the pool, I never really feel like I'm missing my legs," she said. "Instead, I feel like a mermaid."

Jessica became one of the most successful swimmers in Paralympic history. She competed in five Games and won twenty-nine medals, including sixteen gold.

Dr. Guttmann probably had no idea just how big the Paralympics would become. The 2020 Games held in Tokyo had the most participants ever, with more than 4,400 athletes from 163 countries competing in twenty-two different sports. And what do we know about every one of these athletes? They were all spirits in motion—always moving forward.

VIOLET PALMER

First Woman to Officiate an NBA Game

BORN 1964

Refereeing any sport on any level is one of the hardest jobs in sports. No matter what you do, half the players, coaches, and fans are angry with your decisions. Officiating the best basketball players in the world, in front of thousands of excited fans, can be intense. "Even on good calls, refs will still get harassed," former NBA star Kobe Bryant said. "Nobody wants to do what they do. It is too darn hard."

Now imagine being a woman refereeing for men in the NBA. That's what Violet Palmer did. Fierce, confident, and decisive, she was made for the job. "I kind of like the control," Violet said with a smile. "I blow my whistle, and everything just stops."

On October 31, 1997, Violet Palmer became the first Black woman—and the first woman overall—to officiate an NBA game. Violet and another female referee, Dee Kantner, joined the league together that season, but Violet refereed first.

It wasn't easy for Violet. Players yelled bad words at her. They argued when they believed Violet made the wrong call. She even had to break up fights between players, most of whom were over a foot taller and one hundred pounds heavier than she was. But Violet stood up to the players and held her ground.

Violet grew up in Compton, California. She played point guard in high school and at Cal Poly Pomona University, where her team won two NCAA Division II titles. She also began her officiating career in women's hoops soon after she graduated, where she was considered the third-best referee in the world for women's basketball.

Then, the NBA came calling, and Violet could not resist the challenge. She began by officiating NBA summer league games and continued from there. When she retired in 2016, she had worked 919 total games over eighteen seasons. She also officiated nine different postseason games.

"You have to know that you are good at what you do," Violet explained about her career. "Trust me, I am going to get a lot more right calls than I did wrong."

Violet's success made it easier for other women to follow in her shoes. In the 2020–2021 season, six female referees were on the league's full-time officiating staff, and there are no doubt many more to come.

JUSTIN PECK

First Motorsports Racer to Discuss Bipolar Disorder

BORN 1979

Sometimes the challenges an athlete faces are not visible to the fans or to the media. When a difficulty or an injury is physical, it's clear; you might see a splint, bandage, or crutches. Such injuries are considered part of the deal for people in physical activities. But what about when the challenges an athlete faces are mental? For a long time, the sports world did not understand or even acknowledge mental health issues. One athlete became part of the movement to change that.

For years, Justin Peck didn't understand what was going on in his brain. He became very depressed and also had mood swings, where he might suddenly feel intensely sad or extremely excited. School was a challenge, and he was often picked on for acting out. Justin began racing motorcycles when he was seventeen years old; for a while, he had found something that calmed his overactive mind.

"I've always said that the helmet is my medication," he stated. "There's something about being able to put my helmet over my face right before I race that takes away the outside chaos and keeps me focused."

Justin began his long career in off-road racing in his twenties, taking part in numerous races. Off-road races are held on rough, dusty tracks through deserts. The vehicles bounce and jump, and the racers are put through an intense physical ordeal. It's also a tough mental sport, calling for split-second decisions and great courage.

While Justin loved racing, he was still dealing with the mental health challenges from his youth. At one point, he became so depressed he attempted suicide. Finally, when he was twenty-six, he was diagnosed with bipolar disorder and depression. Justin then used the same grit and toughness that had helped him survive more than eighty broken bones in racing accidents to learn to live with his condition.

Justin started taking medication, worked with doctors and therapists, changed his diet, and began to talk and write about his struggles with his mental health. Even as he continued racing motorcycles, dune buggies, and trucks, Justin motivated thousands with speeches and with a book he wrote about his life.

With the support of his children, Justin continues fighting. His condition can sometimes be overwhelming and keep him from racing. But as one of the few professional athletes with bipolar disorder, he knows he can be an example to others, and that helps him keep racing...and keep thriving.

MANON RHÉAUME

First Woman to Play with an NHL Team

BORN 1972

Helping your nation win a world championship is a memorable and important event in any athlete's life. In 1992, Manon Rhéaume (RAY-ohm) did just that as the goalkeeper for the Canadian women's hockey team. But the world championship was not the most memorable thing that happened to her that year. In a preseason NHL game, Manon became the first woman to play for any of the four major North American men's sports leagues when she took the ice for the Tampa Bay Lightning during a preseason game. In the twenty minutes she played, she gave up only two goals!

Being the first wasn't new for Manon, who was born in Quebec in 1972. Her father was a hockey coach, and she grew up playing with and against her two brothers. When she was nineteen years old, she was the first woman to play in a men's junior hockey league in Canada, and later she became the first woman to play for minor-league pro hockey teams in the United States and Canada.

When she was twenty, the Lightning signed her to a contract to give her a shot. Manon and the team knew that the move was mostly for publicity, but she took it very seriously, practicing hard with the team before her big day. She played in one additional game with Tampa Bay in the 1993 preseason. As of 2022, no woman has played in any regular-season games in any of the four major North American men's sports, but Manon came the closest.

Manon continued with the Canadian women's team, winning gold at the 1994 World Championships and silver at the 1998 Winter Olympics. She would occasionally play on some men's minor league teams during those years too.

Manon's hockey life continued after she left the ice in 2000. She was a goalkeeping coach for a Minnesota college. She encouraged young girls to play hockey while helping design and sell hockey gear for girls. And Manon returned briefly in 2008 to her spot in front of the net to play in the Premier Hockey Federation, a pro women's hockey league. She worked with the NHL's Detroit Red Wings as a television reporter, and in 2022, the Los Angeles Kings hired her to help the team's scouting staff develop young players.

Manon's time in the NHL was brief, but it was historic...and inspiring!

FRANK ROBINSON

First Black Manager in MLB

———

1935–2019

When Jackie Robinson spoke, baseball listened. On Opening Day in 1972, Robinson called on baseball to hire a Black person as a manager. Starting with Buck O'Neil in 1962 with the Chicago Cubs, several had acted as coaches over the years, but none had been put in charge. Three years later, Frank Robinson (no relation to Jackie) was named the player-manager for the Cleveland Indians, a team now known as the Guardians.

When Frank got the manager position, he was already one of the most famous and successful players in the game. A powerful slugger, he was the only player to be named the MVP in each pro baseball league (1961 with Cincinnati and 1966 with Baltimore) and won the AL Triple Crown (leading a league in homers, RBI, and batting average) in 1966. Frank was the World Series MVP when the Baltimore Orioles won the title in 1966. Frank also helped the Orioles win the 1970 World Series and played in fourteen All-Star Games. Starting in 1968, he spent his winters as manager of the Santurce Crabbers, a team in Puerto Rico's winter league.

In 1974, Frank was playing for Cleveland as a designated hitter and first baseman. When the team's leadership fired manager Ken Aspromonte, they asked Frank to manage the team.

"I don't think I was hired because I was Black," Robinson said. "I hope not. I think I've been hired because of my ability. The only wish I could have is that Jackie Robinson [who died in 1972] could be here today to see this happen."

On Opening Day in 1975, the fans greeted Frank with a standing ovation when he brought out the team's lineup card. They cheered even louder when he smacked a solo home run in his first at bat as the designated hitter. To cap off his historic day, Cleveland earned a 5–3 victory over the New York Yankees.

It was the start of a career as a manager that was almost as long—but not as successful—as his playing career. Frank ran major-league teams for sixteen years, including the San Francisco Giants, Montreal Expos, and Washington Nationals. He had his best year in 1989 when he was named the AL Manager of the Year while in charge of the Orioles. Frank's managing career began with making history, and his playing career was capped with a spot in the National Baseball Hall of Fame.

JACKIE ROBINSON

First Black Player in MLB

——

1919–1972

Today, more than a third of Major League Baseball players are people of color. They all have Jackie Robinson to thank.

When Jackie jogged onto the field as a Brooklyn Dodger on April 15, 1947, it was one of the biggest days in sports history. Jackie became the first Black player to play in the major leagues in the twentieth century. Before Jackie, major-league owners refused to sign Black players even though they were as good as—if not better than—white players. Black athletes, therefore, played in the segregated, all-Black Negro Leagues.

During this historic season, Jackie faced death threats. Opposing players held their bats like machine guns, pretending to shoot him. They also used their spikes to intentionally step on Jackie when he stood on first base. People in the crowd yelled hateful and racist insults at him. They even threw glass bottles at him.

But Jackie never reacted to these physical and verbal insults. He just answered by playing outstanding baseball. In his first season, Jackie helped the Dodgers win the National League pennant. He batted .297 and stole a league-best twenty-nine bases. He was named Rookie of the Year.

Jackie admitted he almost cracked because fans were so terrible to him. He said he didn't care if anybody liked him or not. He wanted something else.

"All I ask is that you respect me as a human being," he said.

Jackie played for ten seasons in the majors. He helped the Dodgers win five more National League pennants and a World Series title versus the New York Yankees in 1955. Jackie retired in 1956 with a .311 career batting average and 197 stolen bases.

After his retirement, Jackie continued to fight for civil rights off the field. He marched with Martin Luther King Jr. and worked for the National Association for the Advancement of Colored People (NAACP).

In 1962, Jackie was inducted into the National Baseball Hall of Fame. His No. 42 uniform is now retired by Major League Baseball. No player can ever wear this number again—except on April 15. That date is now officially celebrated as Jackie Robinson Day. Every team honors what he did for the game and for others by allowing its players to wear No. 42.

"A life is not important except in the impact it has on others' lives," Jackie famously said. And Jackie's life had a huge impact.

ROBBIE ROGERS

First Openly Gay American Pro Soccer Player

———

BORN 1987

In 2013, when he announced to the world that he is gay, Robbie Rogers feared he would have to give up soccer, the sport he had loved and played since he was a kid. Instead, he returned to the field, becoming the first openly gay male athlete in an American pro sports league. In 2014, he became a champion too, helping the Los Angeles Galaxy win the Major League Soccer (MLS) Cup.

Robbie grew up in California and was a soccer star very early. He played one year at the University of Maryland before joining the Columbus Crew in MLS in 2007 when he was only nineteen years old. He spent five seasons with them, winning his first MLS Cup in 2008 and scoring seven goals in nearly one hundred games. He also played eighteen games for the U.S. National Team, including appearing in the 2008 Olympics.

In 2011, Robbie joined Leeds United, a pro team in England. In 2013, he was with another English team, Stevenage. He felt it was time to let the world know who he was. However, he did it as he was leaving his team, believing he would not be allowed to play as an openly gay man.

After Robbie came out, he told a reporter, "I was very fearful how my teammates were going to react. Even though I'd still be the same person, would it change the way they acted toward me?" He was also worried about how his family would react, but they were super supportive, which was a huge relief.

Rogers was ready to stop playing, but when he came back to the United States, he quickly found a new team. The Galaxy respected him as a quick, smart, solid midfielder; his sexual identity didn't matter. Robbie played four seasons with the Galaxy before retiring in 2016 to pursue other dreams. He got married in 2017 and has two children with his husband, Greg.

The fight against homophobia in men's soccer continues. Some players and fans are still not accepting or welcoming. But on the other hand, many teams now hold Pride Nights and actively encourage gay fans to attend, following the example of women's soccer, which has long been an inclusive and supportive place for gay athletes. As of 2022, more than a dozen pros in men's soccer leagues around the world have come out, inspiring fans and teammates, and continuing to move the sport toward greater equality.

ABBY ROQUE

First Indigenous U.S. Women's Hockey Player

―――

BORN 1997

Abby Roque didn't have to go far to learn how to play hockey. Her dad, Jim, was a coach, and when the winter got cold in their northern Michigan home, he built a hockey rink in the family's frozen backyard. Abby *did* have to travel far to make history, though. In 2022, she went all the way to China for the Winter Olympics, where she became the first Indigenous ice hockey player in the history of Team USA.

Abby's family is part of the Ojibwe First Nations community. While the majority of the Ojibwe people live in Canada, Abby's family settled in Michigan. Abby always knew she wanted hockey to be part of her life. When she was in seventh grade, she wrote a letter that said her goals were to play for the University of Wisconsin and compete in the Olympics. Inspired by her dad and with the experience from her home rink, she started her journey by playing with boys' teams in high school. Her opponents were bigger and stronger, so she became a crafty stick-handler to avoid hard checks. She was soon invited to join national junior women's teams too.

In 2016, Abby made one of her dreams come true when she joined the Wisconsin Badgers. She recalls that some of her college teammates said she was the first Indigenous person they had ever met. Abby starred for Wisconsin for four seasons, scoring at least 40 points in three seasons. The highlight came in the 2018–2019 season when she and the Badgers won the national championship.

In 2022, Abby saw another dream come true when she was selected for the U.S. Olympic team. In seven games in China, she scored a goal and had two assists, helping the U.S. team win a silver medal. In the spring of 2022, she became a pro hockey player and scored the first women's pro hockey goal in the famous Madison Square Garden.

Abby has also become a major advocate for women in sports and for Indigenous representation. "The big thing is just making sure that everybody knows that there's a place in the sport for them and that they shouldn't be intimidated," Roque said. "If you're good enough to play with the boys, play with the boys. And even if they don't think you're good enough to play with them, show them...plain and simple."

WILMA RUDOLPH

First American Woman to Win Three Golds in One Olympics

———

1940–1994

Wilma Rudolph spent most of her childhood sick and in bed. She suffered from scarlet fever, pneumonia, and eventually polio, a virus that causes paralysis. Because of polio, Wilma temporarily lost the use of her left leg when she was six years old, but she still grew up to be the fastest woman in the world.

Wilma was born in St. Bethlehem, Tennessee, and grew up under segregation. She was the twentieth of twenty-two children! Her brothers and sisters took turns massaging Wilma's left leg every day to try and make it better. Because she was Black, the local hospital refused to treat Wilma. So her mother took her to a free physical therapy clinic in Nashville, fifty miles away.

Wilma was able to walk without braces by age nine. In high school, she became a spectacular basketball player; she was so good because she was so fast! The Tennessee State track coach, Ed Temple, saw Wilma play and recruited her to run track for him in college.

While at Tennessee State, Wilma ran in the 1960 Olympics in Rome, Italy. This was the first Games ever broadcasted by American television, and Wilma was the star. Wilma was a graceful runner with incredibly long legs. It seemed like for every step she took, the other runners had to take two or three.

"She looked like this beautiful gazelle just floating through the air," teammate Barbara Jones Slater said about Wilma.

At the Olympics, Wilma easily won the 100- and 200-meter races, and then anchored the U.S. 4 x 100-meter relay team that came in first. This meant Wilma became the first American woman to win three gold medals in one Olympics.

Wilma became a national hero and used her fame to promote civil and women's rights. She refused to attend any segregated events, so a post-Olympic parade and celebration in her honor was the first nonsegregated event in her hometown. She started the Wilma Rudolph Foundation, a not-for-profit organization that helps train young athletes.

"I remind those kids that the triumph cannot be without the struggle," Wilma said.

Wilma's triumph through perseverance inspired Black female Olympians who came after her.

"Gosh, I thought, if she could do it, why can't I do it too?" said Florence Griffith Joyner, a three-time Olympic gold medal winner.

MARLA RUNYAN

First Legally Blind Olympic Runner

BORN 1969

When Marla Runyan was in grade school, she began having trouble seeing. She couldn't decipher the writing on the chalkboard or read any street signs. Marla became frustrated in the classroom because it was so difficult to read, so when she went out to lunchtime recess, she ran. Running made Marla feel better. When she ran, her faulty vision didn't seem to matter anymore.

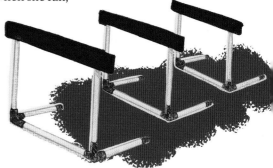

When Marla was nine, she was diagnosed with Stargardt disease, a genetic eye disease that causes progressive vision loss. Marla could make out shapes and colors, but that was about it. Marla learned she would be legally blind for the rest of her life. As a result, running became even more important to her.

Marla ran for her high school track team and then went on to compete at San Diego State University. She participated in the heptathlon, a two-day event made up of 100-meter hurdles, high jump, shot put, 200 meters, long jump, javelin, and 800 meters. She later competed in the 1992 and 1996 Paralympics and won five gold medals and one silver. She soon transitioned to middle distances, where she really began to excel.

Marla became the first legally blind runner to compete in an Olympics. At the 2000 Games in Sydney, Australia, she finished eighth in the 1,500-meter race—the highest finish ever for an American woman in this event.

"I never said I want to be the first legally blind runner to make the Olympics. I just wanted to be an Olympian," Marla said. "I think my vision is just a circumstance that happened, and I don't look at it as a barrier."

Marla became a three-time national champion in the 5,000-meter race. She ran that same distance at the 2004 Olympics in Athens and later became a champion marathoner. When Marla races, she cannot see who she is competing against or even the racing clock. Sometimes after a race, she doesn't know if she won or what place she finished in. But Marla says all this really doesn't matter to her.

"That's why I run," she wrote in her book, *No Finish Line*. "Because it's a way of experiencing the world through sound and touch and movement. I can stand not to see the world, but I can't stand not to move through it."

BILL RUSSELL

First Black NBA Head Coach

———

1934–2022

On and off the basketball court, Bill Russell was a winner. He carried his teams to championships even as he became an inspirational leader. In 1966, he became the first Black head coach in NBA history. This was one of many milestones in his outstanding career.

Bill was born in segregated Louisiana in 1934, and his family moved to Oakland, California, when he was young. Even with a large Black population there, Bill witnessed and was affected by racism. He soon found a home on the basketball court. Tall and strong, he ended up at the University of San Francisco, where he led the team to two national titles in 1955 and 1956. Bill developed into one of the game's best defenders, creating new ways to block shots and stop drives to the basket.

In 1956, Bill joined the NBA's Boston Celtics, where he began a stunning career. He led the NBA in rebounding five times, won five NBA MVP awards, and made twelve All-Star teams. After Boston won nine NBA titles, the team owner and coach Red Auerbach named Bill as the player-coach for the 1966–1967 season. Bill led Boston to two more titles before his playing career ended in 1969.

Off the court, Bill was a winner too. He used his fame to speak out for civil rights. He went to Mississippi in the 1960s to put on basketball clinics for Black children and took part in the March on Washington in 1963. Incredibly, even as he was helping the Celtics win title after title, his home was vandalized by racists. When Bill was the first Black player inducted into the Naismith Memorial Basketball Hall of Fame in 1975, he refused to attend the ceremony because he believed the hall at the time did not do enough for equality in the sport.

Bill coached an additional five NBA seasons, but even after he retired, players continued to visit him, seeking advice and inspiration. In 2009, the NBA named the NBA Finals MVP award after him. And in 2011, President Barack Obama awarded Bill the Presidential Medal of Freedom. Soon after Bill's death in 2022 at the age of eighty-eight, he earned another first: his uniform number, 6, was retired for the entire NBA, something that had never been done before. This was a fitting honor for one of basketball's greatest legends.

A Time for Equality: U.S. WOMEN'S SOCCER TEAM

The U.S. women's national soccer program has a history of awesomeness. They are one of the most successful sports programs in the world, having won four World Cup titles and four Olympic gold medals. More than one billion people watched them beat the Netherlands, 2–0, in the 2019 Women's World Cup soccer tournament.

This legacy of excellence all started with the 1991 national team. That year, the International Federation of Soccer (FIFA) held the first World Cup for women. (Men had been competing in a World Cup every four years since 1930.) The World Cup is the biggest sporting event in the world, with teams competing from all over the globe.

The 1991 tournament was held in Guangdong, China, and twelve teams were invited to compete. The U.S. team bulldozed through their competition, winning six straight matches during the two-week tournament and outscoring their opponents 25–5. In the championship game versus Norway, the two teams were tied, 1–1, with two minutes left in the game. In front of sixty-three thousand fans, American star Michelle Akers stole a pass and scored to win both the game and the World Cup!

"Girls in the United States can now see women playing a high level of soccer," said Akers, who led her team with ten goals across the tournament, "and they can realize, 'Hey, there is a national team, and it's the best in the world.'"

This victory marked the beginning of world domination for the United States. It also kicked off the enthusiasm and excitement for soccer, and in particular women's soccer, in the United States. Since 1991, there has been more than a 200 percent increase in girls' high school soccer participation.

"People around the world have gotten a glimpse of women's football [soccer]," said Andreas Herren, a spokesman for FIFA about the game. "And they can see that it has all the excitement and emotion and joy the men's game has."

Eight years after the first World Cup, the United States hosted the 1999 event. The U.S. team advanced to the final again to face China. Playing in front of more than ninety thousand fans and with a record forty million viewers watching on television,

the Americans won the game in a thrilling shootout, 5–4. Brandi Chastain scored the clinching goal, and her celebration pose was plastered on magazine covers.

Despite their success, the female players were not paid a lot of money by the U.S. Soccer Federation. In fact, the men's team, which had never won a World Cup or an Olympic medal, earned a lot more. Finally in 2022, more than forty years after winning their first World Cup, the team won its lawsuit against the U.S. Soccer Federation for equal pay and is now on the same pay scale as the men's national team.

Team captain Megan Rapinoe was the team's fierce leader who led this fight. Afterward, she said, "Knowing that we're going to leave the game in an exponentially better place than when we found it is everything."

ART SHELL

First Black Head Coach in Modern NFL

BORN 1946

Art Shell was used to knocking people down. As an offensive tackle, he was one of the best blocking linemen in the NFL from 1968 to 1982. He helped the Oakland Raiders win two Super Bowls and was named to eight Pro Bowls. His skill on the field earned him a spot in the Pro Football Hall of Fame in 1989. After his playing career was over, Art knocked down an even bigger barrier: in 1989, the Raiders named Art the first Black head coach in the NFL since 1921. (Fritz Pollard was a player-coach with the Akron Pros in 1921.)

Art got the call from Raiders owner Al Davis late one evening. Davis had owned the team since the early 1960s, so he knew Art well as a player and as one of the team's assistant coaches.

"You understand the Raider way," Davis told his former player. "You're a leader. You're smart. You work hard. Everyone respects you, so you're the perfect choice. Think about it and get some sleep."

Art quickly accepted the historic offer. At a press conference, he said, "I'm proud of [being given the job], but I'm also a Raider. I don't believe the color of my skin entered into this decision. I was chosen because Al Davis felt I was the right person at the right time."

Art led the Raiders for six seasons, winning the NFL Coach of the Year award in 1990 when the team finished 12–4. His overall record in those six seasons was 54–38. He returned to coach one more season in 2006.

While Art led the way in breaking down the barrier, the wall is still high. In Super Bowl XLI (2007), for the first time, both teams were led by Black head coaches—Lovie Smith of Chicago and Tony Dungy of Indianapolis. Rules have been put in place to force teams to interview people of color for all open head coaching jobs. Still, there have been more than five hundred head coaches in NFL history, and as of 2022, only twenty-eight of them have been people of color. In 2022, 70 percent of the NFL's players were Black, but only two of the thirty-two teams had Black head coaches. Looks like there's still some more knocking down to do!

JAMES STEWART JR.

First Black Motorsports National Champion

———

BORN 1985

What has kept Black athletes from succeeding—or even taking part—in motorsports? For a long time, it was overt racism. White-dominated racing series simply did not want or allow Black racers. In more recent years, systemic racism and lack of resources have been a factor, keeping people from tough socioeconomic situations out. But in the early 2000s, a racer came along who broke both of those barriers: James Stewart Jr. revved his motorcycle to the front of the pack in motocross and supercross to become the first Black champion in any American motorsport.

James had a leg up. His father, James Sr., was a pro motocross rider. Motocross racers steer powerful motorcycles over outdoor dirt tracks with lots of jumps, rough ridges, and tight, dust-churning turns. Supercross is similar but takes place on shorter tracks built in stadiums and arenas.

Mentored by his dad, James was a national amateur champion by the time he was seven. His family traveled in a motor home for years to take him to all his races, and he and his brother were homeschooled. By the time he was sixteen, James had won nearly a dozen more national titles. So he decided to turn pro.

The victories continued, and the money poured in. His success and his background made him a national story, with millions of new fans flocking to watch his races, including many who had never followed the sport before. In 2002, James won the 125cc championship, the first national title by a Black racer in any motorsport. He won the supercross title in 2004 and 2007. His biggest year came in 2008 when he was national motocross champ with a perfect season—twenty-four wins in twenty-four races.

Motocross is a tough sport, and James had to battle back from breaking his arm, leg, and collarbone at different points. But he was devoted to the sport and to winning. He used his fame to sign with lots of sponsors, and he made millions for himself and his family.

By the time James retired in 2019, he was second all-time with forty-five supercross and fifty motocross race wins. He also won two world championships in supercross and helped the U.S. team win the Motocross of Nations three times. Few racers have been as dominant as James.

TONI STONE

First Woman to Regularly Play Pro Men's Baseball

———

1921–1996

Baseball player Toni Stone was often told by rude fans and even teammates to "go home and fix your husband some biscuits!"

Toni firmly declined the suggestion. Instead, she kept playing as the first woman on a big-league baseball team. Toni played second base for the Indianapolis Clowns and then the Kansas City Monarchs of the Negro American League.

Toni was born Marcenia Lyle in St. Paul, Minnesota. She loved baseball almost as soon as she could walk. She first got the nickname "Tomboy" because in those days, not many girls played sports. "Tomboy" is a nickname for an athletic girl who likes to do things considered boyish. "Tomboy" eventually turned into "Toni." As a teenager playing baseball on fields near her house, Toni's scrappy athleticism caught the attention of Gabby Street, a former major-league catcher who was managing a Negro minor league team in St. Paul. Gabby bought Toni a pair of cleats and invited her to his baseball camp.

Toni spent years in the minor leagues until she was brought up to the big leagues in 1953. After Jackie Robinson and other Black players left to play in the major leagues, the Negro League was struggling. Syd Pollack, owner of the Clowns, hoped Toni would draw new fans. It worked—for a time. Crowds came out to see if a woman could compete with men. Over two seasons, Toni hit a respectable .243, even connecting for a single off Hall of Fame pitcher Satchel Paige, and proved that she belonged on the field.

The time of Toni's baseball career was hard for all Black players but doubly hard for a Black woman. Toni's teammates weren't nice to her, and when they traveled, she had to find places to stay all on her own. None of that mattered to Toni; she just wanted to play baseball.

Toni was inducted into the International Women's Sports Hall of Fame in 1985 and was honored, along with other Negro League players, by the National Baseball Hall of Fame in 1991. She was also made into a Google Doodle in celebration of Black History Month in 2022. Almost seventy years after Toni entered the big leagues, a play about her life, titled *Toni Stone*, debuted in theaters across the United States. The play, just like the player herself, earned rave reviews.

MAJOR TAYLOR

First Black American to Be a World Sports Champion

———

1878–1932

In the late 1800s and early 1900s, before motorsports began, bicycles ruled the racing world. One athlete was the very best at bike racing—Marshall "Major" Taylor, a Black American.

Born near Indianapolis, the future superstar got his first bike to deliver papers. He soon worked at a bike shop while wearing a military-style uniform, so he was nicknamed Major. The shop's owner pushed him into his first race...and Major won! However, because he was Black in a segregated time, he was not allowed to take part in other races. In 1896, when Major was seventeen, a businessman named Louis Munger helped him show off his speed on a track in Indianapolis. Major broke the local record for a mile, then the world record for one-fifth of a mile. After that, Munger brought Major to work and race for a bike company in Massachusetts, where segregation was far less common.

Major raced on tracks and outdoors, in sprints and six-day-long marathons. He was often struck or pushed by white riders, and he was once attacked by a biker he defeated. Fans threw objects at him as he rode too. But Major kept riding...and winning. In 1899, he was named the world champion, the first Black American athlete to earn a major world sports title.

His supporters urged him to race in Europe, where he would be treated fairly and even earn more prize money. He resisted for two years because most races were held on Sundays. As a devout Baptist, he would not ride on what he considered God's holy day. French organizers wanted him to ride so much that they changed the days some events were held. Major began a worldwide tour that lasted almost until he retired in 1910. He won races in many countries, made more money than just about any athlete in the world

at the time, and was celebrated wherever he went...except in some places in his home country.

When Major died in 1932, he had lost all his money and was buried in an unmarked grave. Cycling fans found out years later and had him reburied in Worcester, Massachusetts, with a proper headstone. A street in the city is named for him, where a statue of him stands, the greatest "unknown" world champion ever.

LIA THOMAS

First Transgender NCAA Champion

———

BORN 1999

On March 17, 2022, swimmer Lia Thomas became the first transgender athlete to win an NCAA national championship. As a swimmer for the University of Pennsylvania, she won the 500-meter freestyle race. Lia's journey to becoming a women's swimming champion wasn't easy, and it wasn't without controversy. When Lia began swimming at Penn, she identified as a man.

Lia grew up swimming in Austin, Texas. As a high schooler, she was one of the top swimmers in the state. After high school, she joined the men's team as a freshman at Penn. As a sophomore, she finished second in three events at the men's Ivy League Championships. By then, Lia felt like she was competing for the wrong team. She was sure she was a woman, not a man. That spring, Lia began hormone therapy, which helped change her body and make it appear more feminine to match who she was inside.

Even though she was transitioning, Lia wanted to keep swimming. With the support of her coaches and teammates, Lia joined the women's team. By doing this, Lia was not breaking any rules: the NCAA allowed trans women to compete on a women's team after they had undergone one year of hormone therapy. By the time Lia began competing, she had already completed two years of therapy.

When Lia began undergoing hormone therapy, her muscles became softer, she gained more fat, and her times in the pool slowed. But she was immediately one of the best female swimmers in the country. She set school, pool, and Ivy League records on her way to winning the national title, and her success resulted in some controversy surrounding her motives.

"People will say, 'She just transitioned so she has an advantage, so she can win,'" Lia said. "I transitioned to be happy, to be true to myself."

Lia faced many critics when she began competing as a woman, but she was brave and fearless through it all. "I just want to show trans kids and younger trans athletes that they're not alone," she said. "They don't have to choose between who they are and the sport they love." Lia is living as her true self, and to her, this is far more important than any championship or trophy could ever be.

JIM THORPE

First Native American Olympic Gold Medalist

———

1887–1953

One of the greatest athletes in American history was not allowed to become an American citizen until he was twenty-nine years old. Jim Thorpe was born in 1887 as a member of the Sac and Fox Nation in Oklahoma. His mother had roots in other Native American nations, while his father was a white man. At that time, people born into Native American nations were not eligible to be American citizens.

That didn't matter to young Jim, though, who simply enjoyed becoming one of the strongest, fastest kids around. He and his friends played and ran in the woods. They swam in rivers and ponds, played games, and picked up sports like football and baseball.

However, Jim's father sent him to a series of boarding schools away from home. Jim did not like them and usually ran back home. Eventually, Jim found a home at the Carlisle Indian Industrial School in Pennsylvania, where coaches guided him into sports. Soon, he was a champion in track and field. He spent summers playing semipro baseball, and he helped the Carlisle football team become one of the country's best. In 1912, he made the U.S. Olympic team in the multisport pentathlon and decathlon. At the games in Stockholm, he dominated the competition, winning gold in both events, the first gold medals ever won by a Native American. The Swedish king called him "the greatest athlete in the world."

Sadly, not long after Jim came back and won again with the Carlisle football team, his Olympic medals were taken away. American sports officials said that his baseball earnings meant he was not an amateur, which was necessary to be in the Olympics back then. Jim was heartbroken and had to leave school.

In 1916, Jim was finally allowed to become an American citizen. He went on to become one of the most multitalented athletes ever. He played six seasons in Major League Baseball, was a champion in pro football, helped form the NFL, and led a traveling basketball team. In 2000, he was named one of the best athletes of the twentieth century.

Many people thought that Jim had been unfairly treated by the Olympics partly because of his heritage, and they fought for years to get his medals back. Jim died in 1953, and it took thirty more years for his family to have his medals returned, and eventually, he was declared a cochampion. In 2022, that status changed, and the Olympic record now shows Jim Thorpe as the only gold medalist of the pentathlon and decathlon in the 1912 Games.

SERENA WILLIAMS

First Player with Career Golden Slams in Singles and Doubles

BORN 1981

Serena Williams revolutionized the sport of women's tennis. She hit the ball harder and served more powerfully than any female player ever. In a sport filled mostly with white athletes, Serena and her sister Venus stood out because they were Black. Serena was bold and brave, on and off the court. In a sport where players were known for wearing polos and simple colors, she wore bright, vivid clothes that showed off her arms. She was defiant and played best when the stakes were highest.

By the time she announced her retirement, Serena had won twenty-three Grand Slam single titles. She was the first tennis player to earn the Golden Slam—winning the Grand Slam and the Olympic gold in both singles and doubles—in the same year. At one point, Serena was ranked number one in the world for 319 straight weeks. That's more than six straight years! In 2022, she was the highest-earning female athlete of all time.

Serena was born in Saginaw, Michigan, but her family moved to Compton, California, soon after her arrival. Serena's father, Richard, watched a tennis match on television and decided he wanted to make his daughters into tennis champions. But the Williams family did not have a lot of money, so Venus and Serena practiced with their father on public tennis courts that had weeds and broken glass. Even in these conditions, Serena took to tennis right away. Both sisters dominated the junior tennis circuit in California, and Serena turned professional when she was only fourteen years old. Three years later, she won the 1999 U.S. Open title. This made her the first Black woman to win a Grand Slam tournament since 1958. In 2002 and 2003, Serena won four Grand Slam titles all in a row, a feat that was called the "Serena Slam."

Serena's fame extended far beyond the tennis world. She crossed into fashion and entertainment, and she became a role model for women, especially Black women. In 2021, a film about Serena's family, *King Richard*, was nominated for Best Picture at the Academy Awards. Serena was a producer on the film.

In 2022, Serena announced she was leaving tennis through the high-fashion magazine *Vogue*. She said she planned to focus on her family and her business, called Serena Ventures. She even bristled when the word *retirement* was used. "We all transform," Serena wrote in her Twitter feed. "Retirement? I prefer forever evolving."

ATOY WILSON

First Black U.S. Figure Skating National Champion

BORN 1951

Atoy Wilson was only fourteen years old when he made history on ice. He became the first Black person to win a U.S. Figure Skating national championship when he came in first in the men's novice division in 1966.

Atoy grew up in Los Angeles, California. He was a gymnast early on. But when he was seven, his mother and father took him to see an ice show, where he discovered he wanted to be a skater too. Atoy thought the moves he used in gymnastics would transfer well into the twists and turns needed for ice skating. He was soon proved right.

Atoy's mom and dad took him to a local rink where Atoy met former professional skater and then coach Mabel Fairbanks. As a competitor, Mabel had been denied entry into skating clubs and competitions because she was a Black woman. But she was determined this was not going to happen to her students. And Mabel saw something special in Atoy. She taught Atoy how to skate but also worked to earn him a spot where she had been denied.

"Mabel was the one who fought in the back rooms, said Atoy, "getting this little Black talented kid out there."

Thanks to Mabel's persistence and Atoy's talent, Atoy became the first Black member of the Los Angeles Figure Skating Club. Before Atoy joined, skating clubs did not allow Black members. As a member of this club, Atoy could now enter competitions. And even though Atoy often felt that judges were harder on him because of the color of his skin, his talent could not be denied.

"He was just very, very smooth at anything there was about skating," said Richard Ewell, another Black figure skater who became a national champion after Atoy. "His spins, his jumps, his edges, his flow—it was just incredible."

Atoy continued to make history as the first Black star of a major ice show. For more than a decade, he went on tour across the United States with *Holiday on Ice* and *Ice Follies*, skating as their lead soloist. By this time, Atoy never felt like he encountered prejudice. "I think skaters and skating fans are too interested in the sport and the skaters to care what a fellow's color is," he said.

TIGER WOODS

First Black Golf Champion in a Major Tournament

——

BORN 1975

Tiger Woods did not just dominate golf; he transcended it. Television ratings quadrupled whenever he competed. The crowds who followed him were enormous. He was the biggest sports star in the world, and he made golf cool. And as a person of color, he changed a sport that had always been dominated by white men.

"They all came to see him; everybody does," explained Dan Kilbridge of *Golfweek*. "When Tiger Woods came to a tournament, he is the tournament."

Tiger burst onto the professional tour in 1997. That year, he became the first African American to win the Masters Tournament in Augusta, Georgia. And Tiger did not just win—he won by a 12-stroke margin, a Masters record. He hit the golf ball farther than any golfer before him, making the Augusta course seem simple. This victory made him the first Black person to win any major golf tournament. The Masters, though, was especially significant. The club did not allow a Black player to compete until 1975 and did not have a Black member until 1990.

"'Train hard, fight easy,' was my mantra growing up," Tiger explained. "I knew I had to be twice as good to be given half the chance."

Tiger Woods began swinging a golf club at eighteen months old. His father, Earl, was of African American, Chinese, and Cherokee descent. His mother, Kultida, was a native of Thailand but also had Chinese and Dutch ancestry.

Tiger played golf for two years at Stanford University and then left school to turn pro. Nike offered him a giant endorsement package. In one of Tiger's first commercials for Nike, the words on the screen read, "There are still courses in the U.S. where I am not allowed to play because of the color of my skin."

Tiger said later, "The Nike ad was just telling the truth."

When Tiger was inducted into the World Golf Hall of Fame in March 2022, he had captured eighty-three PGA Tour wins and fifteen major championships. He was ranked number one in the world for 245 straight weeks. But most importantly, he opened the sport of golf to fans and other players who looked like him.

"Golf had to be shaken up," Tiger said simply.

Thankfully, Tiger was there to lead the charge. But he didn't just shake it up—he completely changed the game and the world surrounding it forever.

BABE ZAHARIAS

First Female Golf Celebrity

1911–1956

Babe was the most diverse female athlete of her time...or maybe the most diverse athlete *of all time*. She just happened to be a woman. This doesn't seem like a big deal now, but when Babe was competing, it was a huge deal. Men and women thought Babe should be at home, making dinner and raising children. But Babe didn't care what people thought. She just wanted to play sports and be the best. She was bold, brash, and confident.

Babe was born Mildred Ella Didrikson in Port Arthur, Texas. She played every sport growing up, including basketball, tennis, swimming, diving, volleyball, and baseball. In Babe's words, she played everything "but dolls." She earned her nickname as a teenager because she reminded the local boys of Babe Ruth, the famous slugger. She starred on her high school's basketball team and then started running track. Even Babe Ruth didn't do all these sports!

After high school, Babe played basketball on an all-women's American team from 1930 to 1932. But she soon returned to track and field. At the 1932 Amateur Athletic Union National track and field championships, Babe won five events and tied for first in a sixth. Babe was competing as a solo performer against teams that had as many as twenty-two members. Her point total beat them all.

Babe won two gold medals at the 1932 Olympics, setting world records in the javelin and hurdles. This was the first gold medal ever awarded to women in the javelin. She won a silver medal in the women's high jump and would have earned gold if the official hadn't ruled that she went over the bar the wrong way.

Babe also boxed. She played on an all-men's baseball team and pitched against major leaguers during spring training in 1934. She was even an expert bowler.

Babe soon turned to golf and focused on that sport for the rest of her career. Known for being able to drive the ball as far as the men, Babe won thirty-one pro tournaments, including ten majors. She founded the Ladies Professional Golf Association and became the first female golf celebrity, winning the U.S. Women's Open in 1948, 1950, and 1954.

Babe was named the Associated Press's Athlete of the Year six times. In 1950, they also named her the world's greatest athlete of the first half of the twentieth century. In 2011, a biography about Babe's life was published. The title, *Wonder Girl*, was the perfect tribute to this barrier-breaking woman.

An Overdue Opportunity: HAUDENOSAUNEE LACROSSE TEAM

How would you feel if your people invented a sport...but then you were not allowed to play it? For many years, that was the story of the Haudenosaunee people and the sport of lacrosse. Sometimes known as the Iroquois, the Haudenosaunee are a group of six Indigenous nations in the northeastern United States and southern Canada: Cayuga, Mohawk, Oneida, Onondaga, Seneca, and Tuscarora. More than a thousand years ago, their ancestors invented a sport they called *dehoñtjihgwa'és*. In the 1700s, French missionaries thought the sticks used in the game resembled a staff carried by Catholic bishops, called *la crosse*.

For the Haudenosaunee, lacrosse is more than a game. It is a part of their spiritual life. Over the centuries, it was played for fun, as practice for battle, and as part of spiritual ceremonies.

By the mid-1800s, nonnative Canadians and Americans had adopted the sport too. Haudenosaunee teams played against them, often winning. In 1880, however, Haudenosaunee teams were banned from international events—kicked out, for racist reasons, of the sport they had created.

The Haudenosaunee kept playing, of course. They played games among themselves, while young people still learned the sport and its place in the culture. In the 1950s, a national team was formed with players from the six nations. This team took part in tournaments in the United States and Canada but still could not travel to international events.

Some of the best Haudenosaunee players also took their skills to college and pro teams in the United States and Canada. Lyle Thompson of the Onondaga is one of the best lacrosse players ever and the only Indigenous person to be the MVP in Major League Lacrosse. Many others were all-stars in indoor and outdoor lacrosse.

The Haudenosaunee national team continued to try to get recognized by World Lacrosse but was repeatedly turned down. International officials did not consider the Haudenosaunee to be a separate or "sovereign" nation. In 1990, after many years of struggle, the Haudenosaunee were finally allowed into world competitions. They became the first team of athletes representing Indigenous people in international sports. Their first

event was the World Games held in Australia in 1990. They finished third at the world championships in 2014 and 2018. The women's team was in the top ten at the 2022 world championship.

However, in 2020, incredibly, the problem happened all over again. The World Games did not invite the Haudenosaunee. Even though the event was in Alabama, the organizers did not see the Haudenosaunee passports as the same as those issued by other nations. When the news broke, the lacrosse world reacted quickly. More than fifty thousand players signed a petition demanding that the team be added.

Ireland's national teams heard about the problem, and they stepped aside to let the Haudenosaunee take part. "None of us would be going to the World Games if it wasn't for the [Haudenosaunee] giving us the gift of their medicine game," said Ireland Lacrosse's Sonny Campbell. The Haudenosaunee men's team finished sixth at the 2022 World Games, while the women's team finished fifth. But winning was only one goal; the goal of reclaiming their place in the sport was accomplished.

A New Vision: SOUTH AFRICAN RUGBY TEAM

This book aims to highlight many athletes, beyond the most famous like Jackie Robinson, who were fearless and first in the world of sports. Learning about these courageous people and teams shows how far the world has come…and how far we still have to go. But through it all, we see the power of sports to help change the world, to let everyone play, no matter what.

In this book, we've focused on American sports, but discrimination in sports was not limited to the United States. For decades, people around the world have been prevented from taking part in sports because of their race, gender, or sexuality. Below is the story of a famous fearless first that still matters today and shows how sports have the power to heal.

For most of the twentieth century, South Africa was a segregated country. White people with roots in England and the Netherlands were in control of a nation that was 70 percent Black. In the 1940s, the government passed a series of laws that split the country. Policies called apartheid (uh-PART-ide) created two South Africas, one for whites and one for Blacks. Black people protested, but the police cracked down and thousands went to jail, including a young protestor named Nelson Mandela.

Over the next few decades, the world sports community played a part in trying to get these racist laws changed. Soccer's FIFA kicked South Africa out in 1963. The International Olympic Committee took the planned Summer Games away from the country in 1964—South African teams could not take part in the Olympics for many years. International groups in charge of basketball, gymnastics, judo, and others all banned the nation due to apartheid. Sports was doing its part to show that racism was wrong.

Then in the early 1990s, everything changed in South Africa. After getting out of prison, Nelson Mandela led talks to end apartheid. In 1994, he was elected president. The rules in the country changed, and the sports world began to let South Africans back in. The Rugby World Cup was even played there in 1995.

The hard-hitting sport of rugby was beloved by South Africa's white population. So how could people root for their national team in the World Cup when it was seen as a white person's sport? In fact, as the tournament began, Black South Africans actively rooted against South Africa's team. But here's where Mandela saw a way to use sports to heal: he chose to embrace and support the team. He encouraged them to add the

nation's first Black World Cup player, Chester Williams. With the assistance of team captain Francois Pienaar, Mandela helped unite a divided country through rugby.

South Africa surprised many by defeating the world's top teams in a series of upsets. Slowly, Black South Africans began to cheer for the team. Mandela was the biggest cheerleader of all. Finally in front of its home fans, in one of the most inspiring wins in the sport's history, an underdog South African team won the World Cup 15–12 over Australia. Mandela handed the championship trophy to Pienaar, a scene unthinkable only a decade earlier.

Did sports solve the problem of racism in South Africa? Not at all. But sports became a stage where the hard-fought unity could be shown and celebrated.

ATHLETES THROUGH THE YEARS

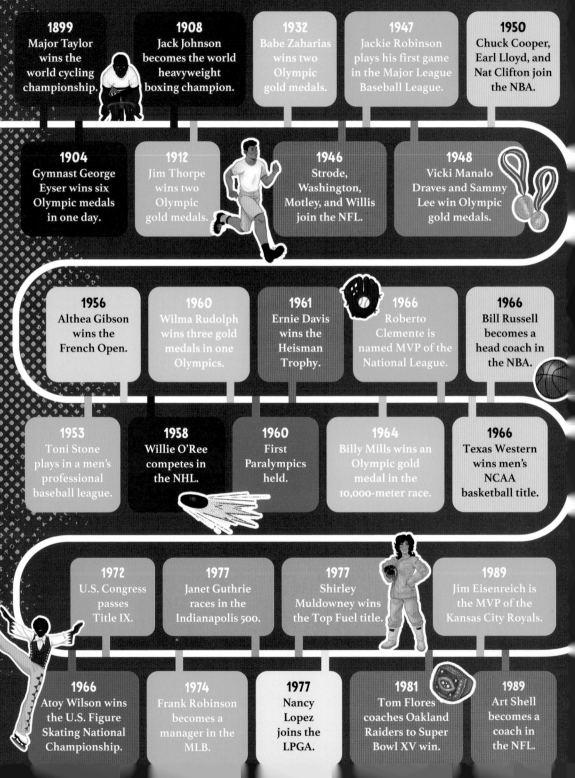

1899 Major Taylor wins the world cycling championship.

1908 Jack Johnson becomes the world heavyweight boxing champion.

1932 Babe Zaharias wins two Olympic gold medals.

1947 Jackie Robinson plays his first game in the Major League Baseball League.

1950 Chuck Cooper, Earl Lloyd, and Nat Clifton join the NBA.

1904 Gymnast George Eyser wins six Olympic medals in one day.

1912 Jim Thorpe wins two Olympic gold medals.

1946 Strode, Washington, Motley, and Willis join the NFL.

1948 Vicki Manalo Draves and Sammy Lee win Olympic gold medals.

1956 Althea Gibson wins the French Open.

1960 Wilma Rudolph wins three gold medals in one Olympics.

1961 Ernie Davis wins the Heisman Trophy.

1966 Roberto Clemente is named MVP of the National League.

1966 Bill Russell becomes a head coach in the NBA.

1953 Toni Stone plays in a men's professional baseball league.

1958 Willie O'Ree competes in the NHL.

1960 First Paralympics held.

1964 Billy Mills wins an Olympic gold medal in the 10,000-meter race.

1966 Texas Western wins men's NCAA basketball title.

1972 U.S. Congress passes Title IX.

1977 Janet Guthrie races in the Indianapolis 500.

1977 Shirley Muldowney wins the Top Fuel title.

1989 Jim Eisenreich is the MVP of the Kansas City Royals.

1966 Atoy Wilson wins the U.S. Figure Skating National Championship.

1974 Frank Robinson becomes a manager in the MLB.

1977 Nancy Lopez joins the LPGA.

1981 Tom Flores coaches Oakland Raiders to Super Bowl XV win.

1989 Art Shell becomes a coach in the NFL.

1990
Haudenosaunee lacrosse team plays in World Games.

1993
Julie Krone wins a Triple Crown race.

1995
South Africa wins the World Cup in rugby.

1997
Violet Palmer officiates an NBA game.

2000
Marla Runyan finishes eighth in the Olympic 1,500-meter race.

1991
U.S. women win World Cup of soccer.

1992
Manon Rheaume plays in an NHL preseason game.

1993
Jim Abbott pitches a no-hitter for New York Yankees.

1997
Golfer Tiger Woods wins his first Masters Tournament.

2002
James Stewart wins the 125cc national motorcycle racing title.

2005
Clay Marzo wins a national surfing title.

2012
Jeremy Lin's scoring binge in the NBA leads to instant fame.

2013
Jason Collins comes out as the first openly gay NBA player.

2014
Tina Ament completes the Ironman World Championship.

2016
Simone Biles wins four gold medals in a single Olympics.

2012
Gabby Douglas becomes an Olympic gymnastics individual all-around champion.

2012
Kyle Maynard climbs Mount Kilimanjaro without assistance.

2013
Robbie Rogers comes out as the first openly gay American soccer player.

2014
Mo'ne Davis plays in the Little League World Series.

2017
Justin Peck reveals his bipolar disorder.

2022
Erin Jackson wins a gold medal in the Winter Olympics.

2022
Rachel Balkovec is hired as manager of the Tampa Tarpons.

2022
Lia Thomas wins an NCAA championship.

2016
Ibtihaj Muhammad wins an Olympic bronze medal.

2020
Becky Hammon coaches one game in the NBA.

2022
Kim Ng becomes the GM of the Miami Marlins.

2022
Abby Roque plays for the U.S. national hockey team.

2022
Serena Williams retires after winning twenty-three career grand slam titles!

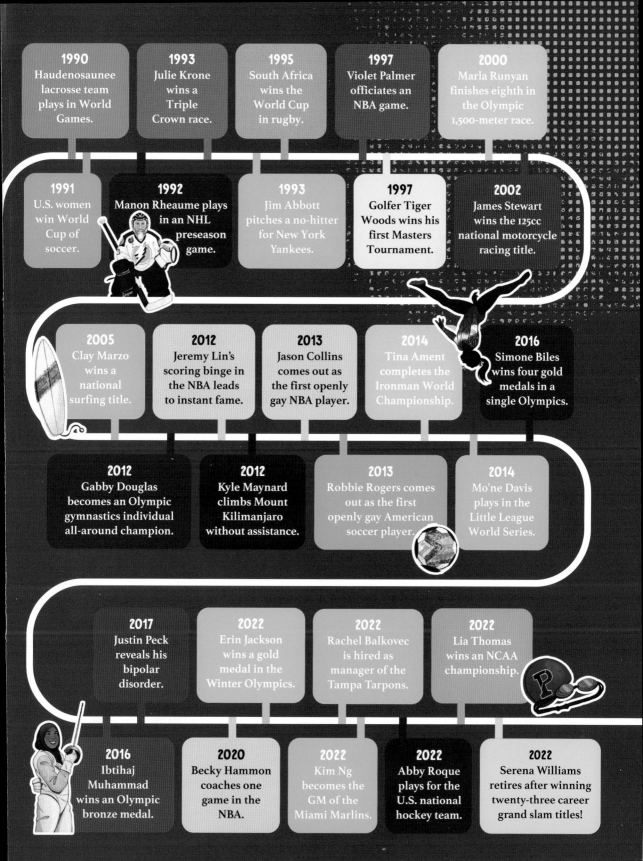

Find Out More!

Check out these books to discover more about some of the athletes mentioned in this book and learn about others who broke barriers and made history!

Black Jack: The Ballad of Jack Johnson by Charles R. Smith Jr. (Square Fish, 2022).

Courage to Soar: A Body in Motion, a Life in Balance by Simone Biles and Michelle Burford (Zondervan, 2016).

Girls with Guts! The Road to Breaking Barriers and Bashing Records by Debbie Gonzales (Charlesbridge, 2019).

An Indigenous Peoples' History of the United States for Young People by Roxanne Dunbar-Ortiz (Beacon Press, 2019).

James Stewart by Jeff Savage (LernerClassroom, 2007).

Just Add Water: A Surfing Savant's Journey with Asperger's by Clay Marzo (Houghton Mifflin Harcourt, 2015).

Let Me Play: The Story of Title IX: The Law That Changed the Future of Girls in America by Karen Blumenthal (Atheneum Books for Young Readers, 2005).

Major Taylor, Champion Cyclist by Lesa Cline-Ransome (Atheneum Books for Young Readers, 2012).

Nancy Lopez: Golf Hall of Famer by Anne Wallace Sharp (Lucent Books, 2008).

The National Team: The Inside Story of the Women Who Changed Soccer by Caitlin Murray (Harry N. Abrams, 2019).

No Excuses: The True Story of a Congenital Amputee Who Became a Champion in Wrestling and in Life by Kyle Maynard (Regnery Publishing, 2006).

Proud: My Fight for an Unlikely American Dream by Ibtihaj Muhammad (Legacy Lit, 2018).

Rebel Girls Champions: 25 Tales of Unstoppable Athletes (Rebel Girls, 2021).

Remember My Name: My Story from First Pitch to Game Changer by Mo'ne Davis (HarperCollins, 2016).

Unstoppable: How Jim Thorpe and the Carlisle Indian School Football Team Defeated Army by Art Coulson (Capstone Editions, 2018).

What Are the Paralympic Games? by Gail Herman (Penguin Workshop, 2020).

Who Is Megan Rapinoe? by Stephanie Loh (Penguin Workshop, 2023).

Who Was Roberto Clemente? by James Buckley Jr. (Penguin Workshop, 2014).

Willie: The Game-Changing Story of the NHL's First Black Player by Willie O'Ree (Viking Press, 2020).

Women in Sports: 50 Fearless Athletes Who Played to Win by Rachel Ignotofsky (Ten Speed Press, 2017).

A Message from the Authors

Telling the stories of these amazing athletes is a privilege. These competitors overcame prejudice and outright discrimination to make the world of sports a more welcoming and inclusive venue for all. Each of them was the first to achieve greatness in their own way, and in turn, their courage paved the way for others to follow.

One of the most exciting parts of writing a book like this is that we know there are even *more* fearless athletes waiting to be discovered. There will always be new competitors setting records, winning championships, and achieving more firsts. Who knows? You might be one of them!

This is why we wanted to ask you for help. Keep an eye out for all these athletes who continue to break through barriers. Share their stories with your friends and family. Athletic arenas are filled with fearless competitors to celebrate. Let's continue to do so together!

About the Authors

Photo © Patty Kelley

James Buckley Jr. is one of the country's most prolific writers of sports and nonfiction for kids, with more than two hundred titles to his name, including twenty in the *New York Times*–bestselling *Who Was...?* biography series, nine books in the *Show Me History* graphic nonfiction series, and fifteen years of writing the *Scholastic Year in Sports*.

A former editor with *Sports Illustrated* and NFL Publishing, James runs Shoreline Publishing Group, a leading producer of nonfiction kids' books for national and school-library publishers. He lives in Santa Barbara, California, where he helps run the Santa Barbara Foresters, the ten-time national champion summer wood-bat baseball team, and plays goalie for an adult soccer team, the Renegades.

Photo © Jeff Labrecque

Ellen Labrecque has written over one hundred nonfiction books for children. She has authored ten biographies in the *New York Times*–bestselling *Who Was...?* biography series, including bios on David Beckham, Kobe Bryant, and Shaquille O'Neal. She enjoys exploring various topics and has channeled this research into other books on sports, outer space, animals, jungles, and the environment.

Ellen grew up outside Philadelphia as a member of a die-hard Phillies and Eagles family. Much to her chagrin, she now lives in a split home with New York sports fans. An athlete herself, Ellen played basketball and lacrosse in college. She has since retired her high tops and cleats for jogging sneakers.

Ellen was a writer and editor at *Sports Illustrated Kids* magazine for nine years, writing profiles on athletes and covering the Olympics and other sporting events. She now writes from her Bucks County, Pennsylvania, home with her family and her dog Oscar (a definite Phillies fan).